Soccer in Sun and Shadow

EDUARDO GALEANO

Translated by
Mark Fried

NATION
BOOKS
New York

Published by Nation Books, A Member of the Perseus Books Group
116 East 16th Street, 8th Floor, New York, NY 10003

Nation Books is a co-publishing venture of
the Nation Institute and the Perseus Books Group.

Books published by Nation Books are available at special discounts for
bulk purchases in the United States by corporations, institutions, and
other organizations. For more information, please contact the Special
Markets Department at the Perseus Books Group, 2300 Chestnut
Street, Suite 200, Philadelphia, PA 19103, or call (800) 255-1514,
or e-mail *special.markets@perseusbooks.com*.

Library of Congress Cataloging-in-Publication Data
Galeano, Eduardo, 1940-
[Futbol a sol y sombra. English]
Soccer in sun and shadow / Eduardo Galeano.
pages cm
Includes bibliographical references and index.
ISBN 978-1-56858-494-2 (pbk.)—
ISBN 978-1-56858-956-5 (e-book) 1. Soccer—History.
2. Soccer—Anecdotes. 3. Soccer—Social aspects. I. Title.
GV942.5.G35 2013
796.334—dc23
2013021572

4 5 6 7 8 9 10

Soccer in Sun and Shadow

ALSO BY EDUARDO GALEANO:

Open Veins of Latin America
Days and Nights of Love and War
Memory of Fire Vol. 1–3
The Book of Embraces
We Say No
Walking Words
Upside Down
Voices of Time
Mirrors
Children of the Days

Contents

vi

viii

Müller	165
Havelange	166
The Owners of the Ball	168
Jesus	173
The 1978 World Cup	174
Happiness	177
Goal by Gemmill	179
Goal by Bettega	180
Goal by Sunderland	181
The 1982 World Cup	182
Pears from an Elm	185
Platini	187
Pagan Sacrifices	188
The 1986 World Cup	192
The Telecracy	195
Staid and Standardized	198
Running Drugstores	200
Chants of Scorn	201
Anything Goes	203
Indigestion	207
The 1990 World Cup	208
Goal by Rincón	210
Hugo Sánchez	211
The Cricket and the Ant	213
Gullit	214
Parricide	216
Goal by Zico	217
A Sport of Evasion	218
The 1994 World Cup	222

x

The pages that follow are dedicated to the children who once upon a time, years ago, crossed my path on Calella de la Costa. They had been playing soccer and were singing:

We lost, we won,
either way we had fun

This book owes much to the enthusiasm and patience of "El Pepe" Barrientos, "Manolo" Epelbaum, Ezequiel Fernández-Moores, Karl Hubener, Franklin Morales, Ángel Ruocco, and Klaus Schuster, who read each draft, caught mistakes, and came up with valuable ideas and information.

Also of great assistance were the critical eye of my wife, Helena Villagra, and the soccer memory of my father, "El Baby" Hughes. My son Claudio and a few friends, or friends of my friends, did their part bringing me books and newspapers or answering queries: Hugo Alfaro, "Zé" Fernando Balbi, Chico Buarque, Nicolás Buenaventura Vidal, Manuel Cabieses, Jorge Consuegra, Pierre Charasse, Julián García-Candau, José González Ortega, "Pancho" Graells, Jens Lohmann, Daniel López D'Alessandro, Sixto Martínez, Juan Manuel Martín Medem, Gianni Minà, Dámaso Murúa, Felipe Nepomuceno, "El Migue" Nieto-Solís, Luis Niño, Luis Ocampos Alonso, Carlos Ossa, Norberto Pérez, Silvia Peyrou, Miguel Ángel Ramírez, Alastair Reid, Affonso Romano de Sant'Anna, Pilar Royo, Rosa Salgado, Giuseppe Smorto, and Jorge Valdano. Osvaldo Soriano collaborated at my invitation.

I ought to say that all of them are innocent of the result, but the truth is I think they are rather guilty for having gotten themselves into this mess.

Author's Confession

Like all Uruguayan children, I wanted to be a soccer player. And I played quite well. In fact I was terrific, but only at night when I was asleep. During the day I was the worst wooden leg ever to set foot on the little soccer fields of my country.

As a fan I also left a lot to be desired. Juan Alberto Schiaffino and Julio César Abbadie played for Peñarol, the enemy team. I was a loyal Nacional fan and I did everything I could to hate them. But with his masterful passes "El Pepe" Schiaffino orchestrated the team's plays as if he were watching from the highest tower of the stadium, and "El Pardo" Abbadie, running in his seven-league boots, would slide the ball all the way down the white touchline, swaying back and forth without ever grazing the ball or his opponents. I couldn't help admiring them, and I even felt like cheering.

Years have gone by and I've finally learned to accept myself for who I am: a beggar for good soccer. I go about the world, hand outstretched, and in the stadiums I plead: "A pretty move, for the love of God."

And when good soccer happens, I give thanks for the miracle and I don't give a damn which team or country performs it.

Soccer

The history of soccer is a sad voyage from beauty to duty. When the sport became an industry, the beauty that blossoms from the joy of play got torn out by its very roots. In this fin de siècle world, professional soccer condemns all that is useless, and useless means not profitable. Nobody earns a thing from the crazy feeling that for a moment turns a man into a child playing with a balloon, a cat toying with a ball of yarn, a ballet dancer flying through the air with a ball as light as a balloon or a ball of yarn, playing without even knowing he's playing, with no purpose or clock or referee.

Play has become spectacle, with few protagonists and many spectators, soccer for watching. And that spectacle has become one of the most profitable businesses in the world, organized not to facilitate play but to impede it. The technocracy of professional sport has managed to impose a soccer of lightning speed and brute strength, a soccer that negates joy, kills fantasy, and outlaws daring.

Luckily, on the field you can still see, even if only once in a long while, some insolent rascal who sets aside the script and commits the blunder of dribbling past the entire opposing side, the referee, and the crowd in the stands, all for the carnal delight of embracing the forbidden adventure of freedom.

The Player

Panting, he runs up the wing. On one side awaits heaven's glory; on the other, ruin's abyss.

He is the envy of the neighborhood: the professional athlete who escaped the factory or the office and gets paid to have fun. He won the lottery. And even if he has to sweat buckets, with no right to failure or fatigue, he gets into the papers and on TV. His name is on the radio, women swoon over him, and children yearn to be like him. But he started out playing for pleasure in the dirt streets of the slums, and now he plays out of duty in stadiums where he has no choice but to win or to win.

Businessmen buy him, sell him, lend him and he lets it all happen in return for the promise of more fame and more money. The more successful he is and the more money he makes, the more of a prisoner he becomes. Forced to live by military discipline, he suffers the punishing daily round of training and the bombardments of painkillers and cortisone that hide his aches and fool his body. And on the eve of big matches, they lock him up in a concentration camp where he does forced labor, eats tasteless food, gets drunk on water, and sleeps alone.

In other human trades, decline comes with old age, but a soccer player can be old at thirty. Muscles tire early: "That guy couldn't score if the field were on a slope."

"Him? Not even if they tied the keeper's hands."

Or before thirty if the ball knocks him out, or bad luck tears a muscle, or a kick breaks a bone and it can't be fixed. And one rotten day the player discovers he has bet his life on a single card and his money is gone and so is his fame. Fame, that fleeting lady, did not even leave him a Dear John letter.

The Goalkeeper

They also call him doorman, keeper, goalie, bouncer, or net-minder. But he could just as well be called martyr, pay-all, penitent, or punching bag. They say where he walks the grass never grows.

He is alone, condemned to watch the match from afar. Never leaving the goal, his only company the two posts and the crossbar, he awaits his own execution by firing squad. He used to dress in black, like the referee. Now the referee doesn't have to dress like a crow and the goalkeeper can console himself in his solitude with colorful gear.

He does not score goals; he is there to keep them from being scored. The goal is soccer's fiesta: the striker sparks delight and the goalkeeper, a wet blanket, snuffs it out.

He wears the number one on his back. The first to be paid? No, the first to pay. It is always the keeper's fault. And when it isn't, he still gets blamed. Whenever a player commits a foul, the keeper is the one who gets punished: they abandon him in the immensity of the empty net to face his executioner alone. And when the team has a bad afternoon, he is the one who pays the bill, expiating the sins of others under a rain of flying balls.

The rest of the players can blow it once in a while or often, and then redeem themselves with a spectacular dribble, a masterful pass, a well-placed volley. Not him. The crowd never forgives the goalkeeper. Was he drawn out by a fake? Left looking ridiculous? Did the ball skid? Did his fingers of steel turn to putty? With a single slip-up the goalie can ruin a match or lose a championship, and the fans suddenly forget all his feats and condemn him to eternal disgrace. Damnation will follow him to the end of his days.

The Idol

A nd one fine day the goddess of the wind kisses the foot of man—that mistreated, scorned foot—and from that kiss the soccer idol is born. He is born in a straw crib in a tin-roofed shack and he enters the world clinging to a ball.

From the moment he learns to walk, he knows how to play. In his early years he brings joy to the sandlots, plays like crazy in the back alleys of the slums until night falls and you can't see the ball, and in his early manhood he takes flight and the stadiums fly with him. His acrobatic art draws multitudes, Sunday after Sunday, from victory to victory, ovation to ovation.

The ball seeks him out, knows him, needs him. She rests and rocks on the top of his foot. He caresses her and makes her speak, and in that tête-à-tête millions of mutes converse. The nobodies, those condemned to always be nobodies, feel they are somebodies for a moment by virtue of those one-two passes, those dribbles that draw Z's on the grass, those incredible backheel goals or overhead volleys. When he plays, the team has twelve players: "Twelve? It has fifteen! Twenty!"

The ball laughs, radiant, in the air. He brings her down, puts her to sleep, showers her with compliments, dances with her. Seeing such things never before seen, his admirers pity their unborn grandchildren who will never see them.

But the idol is an idol for only a moment, a human eternity, all of nothing. And when the time comes for the golden foot to become a lame duck, the star will have completed his journey from burst of light to black hole. His body has more patches than a clown's costume, and by now the acrobat is a cripple, the artist a beast of burden: "Not with your clodhoppers!"

The fountain of public adulation becomes the lightning rod of public rancor: "You mummy!"

Sometimes the idol does not fall all at once. And sometimes when he breaks, people devour the pieces.

The Fan

Once a week, the fan flees his house for the stadium. Banners wave and the air resounds with noisemakers, firecrackers, and drums; it rains streamers and confetti. The city disappears, its routine forgotten. All that exists is the temple. In this sacred place, the only religion without atheists puts its divinities on display. Although the fan can contemplate the miracle more comfortably on TV, he prefers to make the pilgrimage to this spot where he can see his angels in the flesh doing battle with the demons of the day.

Here the fan shakes his handkerchief, gulps his saliva, swallows his bile, eats his cap, whispers prayers and curses, and suddenly lets loose a full-throated scream, leaping like a flea to hug the stranger at his side cheering the goal. While the pagan mass lasts, the fan is many. Along with thousands of other devotees he shares the certainty that we are the best, that all referees are crooked, that all our adversaries cheat.

Rarely does the fan say, "My club plays today." He says, "We play today." He knows it is "player number twelve" who stirs up the winds of fervor that propel the ball when she falls asleep, just as the other eleven players know that playing without their fans is like dancing without music.

When the match is over, the fan, who has not moved from the stands, celebrates *his* victory: "What a goal we scored!" "What a beating we gave them!" Or he cries over *his* defeat: "They swindled us again." "Thief of a referee." And then the sun goes down and so does the fan. Shadows fall over the emptying stadium. On the concrete terracing, a few fleeting bonfires burn, while the lights and voices fade. The stadium is left alone and the fan too returns to his solitude: to the I who had been we. The fan goes off, the crowd breaks up and melts away, and Sunday becomes as melancholy as Ash Wednesday after the death of Carnival.

The Fanatic

The fanatic is a fan in a madhouse. His mania for denying all evidence finally upended whatever once passed for his mind, and the remains of the shipwreck spin about aimlessly in waters whipped by a fury that gives no quarter.

The fanatic shows up at the stadium prickling with strident and aggressive paraphernalia, wrapped in the team flag, his face painted the colors of his beloved team's shirt; on the way he makes a lot of noise and a lot of fuss. He never comes alone. In the midst of the rowdy crowd, dangerous centipede, this cowed man will cow others, this frightened man becomes frightening. Omnipotence on Sunday exorcises the obedient life he leads the rest of the week: the bed with no desire, the job with no calling, or no job at all. Liberated for a day, the fanatic has much to avenge.

In an epileptic fit he watches the match but does not see it. His arena is the stands. They are his battleground. The mere presence of a fan of the other side constitutes an inexcusable provocation. Good is not violent by nature, but Evil leaves it no choice. The enemy, always in the wrong, deserves a thrashing. The fanatic cannot let his mind wander because the enemy is everywhere, even in that quiet spectator who at any moment might offer the opinion that the rival team is playing fairly. Then he'll get what he deserves.

The Goal

The goal is soccer's orgasm. And like orgasms, goals have become an ever less frequent occurrence in modern life.

Half a century ago, it was a rare thing for a match to end scoreless: 0–0, two open mouths, two yawns. Now the eleven players spend the entire match hanging from the crossbar, trying to stop goals, and they have no time to score them.

The excitement unleashed whenever the white bullet makes the net ripple might appear mysterious or crazy, but remember, the miracle does not happen often. The goal, even if it be a little one, is always a goooooooooooooooooooooooal in the throat of the commentators, a "do" sung from the chest that would leave Caruso forever mute, and the crowd goes nuts and the stadium forgets that it is made of concrete and breaks free of the earth and flies through the air.

⚽ ⚽ ⚽ ⚽ ⚽ ⚽ ⚽ ⚽ ⚽ ⚽ ⚽ ⚽ ⚽ ⚽

The Referee

In Spanish he is the *árbitro* and he is arbitrary by definition. An abominable tyrant who runs his dictatorship without opposition, a pompous executioner who exercises his absolute power with an operatic flourish. Whistle between his lips, he blows the winds of inexorable fate to allow a goal or to disallow one. Card in hand, he raises the colors of doom: yellow to punish the sinner and oblige him to repent, and red to force him into exile.

The linesmen, who assist but do not rule, look on from the side. Only the referee steps onto the playing field, and he is certainly right to cross himself when he first appears before the roaring crowd. His job is to make himself hated. The only universal sentiment in soccer: everybody hates him. He gets only catcalls, never applause.

Nobody runs more. This interloper, whose panting fills the ears of all twenty-two players, is obliged to run the entire match without pause. He breaks his back galloping like a horse, and in return for his pains the crowd howls for his head. From beginning to end he sweats oceans chasing the white ball that skips back and forth between the feet of everyone else. Of course he would love to play but never has he been offered that privilege. When the ball hits him by chance, the entire stadium curses his mother. But even so, he is willing to suffer insults, jeers, stones, and damnation just to be there in that sacred green space where the ball floats and glides.

Sometimes, though rarely, his judgment coincides with the inclinations of the fans, but not even then does he emerge unscathed. The losers owe their loss to him and the winners triumph in spite of him. Scapegoat for every error, cause of every misfortune, the fans would have to invent him if he did not already exist. The more they hate him, the more they need him.

For over a century the referee dressed in mourning. For whom? For himself. Now he wears bright colors to disguise his distress.

⑨ ⑨ ⑨ ⑨ ⑨ ⑨ ⑨ ⑨ ⑨ ⑨ ⑨ ⑨ ⑨ ⑨

The Manager

In the old days there was the trainer and nobody paid him much heed. He died without a word when the game stopped being a game and professional soccer required a technocracy to keep the players in line. That was when the manager was born. His mission: to prevent improvisation, restrict freedom, and maximize the productivity of the players, who were now obliged to become disciplined athletes.

The trainer used to say, "Let's play."

The manager says, "Let's go to work."

Today they talk in numbers. The history of soccer in the twentieth century, a journey from daring to fear, is a trip from the 2–3–5 to the 5–4–1 by way of the 4–3–3 and the 4–4–2. Any ignoramus could translate that much with a little help, but the rest is impossible. The manager dreams up formulas as mysterious as the Immaculate Conception, which he uses to develop tactical schemes as indecipherable as the Holy Trinity.

From the old blackboard to the electronic screen: now great plays are planned by computer and taught by video. These dream maneuvers are rarely shown when the matches are broadcast. Television prefers to focus on the furrows in the manager's brow. We see him gnawing his fists or shouting instructions that would certainly turn the match around if anyone could understand them.

Journalists pepper him with questions at the postmatch press conference but he never reveals the secrets of his victories, although he formulates admirable explanations of his defeats. "The instructions were clear, but they didn't listen," he says when the team suffers a big loss to a crummy rival. Or he dispels any doubts by talking about himself in the third person, more or less like this: "The reverses the team suffered today will never mar the achievement of a conceptual clarity that this manager once described as a synthesis of the many sacrifices required to become truly effective."

The machinery of spectacle grinds up everything in its path, nothing lasts very long, and the manager is as disposable as any other product of consumer society. Today the crowd screams, "Never die!" and next Sunday they invite him to kill himself.

The manager believes soccer is a science and the field a laboratory, but the genius of Einstein and the subtlety of Freud is not enough for the owners and the fans. They want a miracle worker like Our Lady of Lourdes, with the stamina of Gandhi.

The Theater

The players in this show act with their legs for an audience of thousands or millions who watch from the stands or their living rooms with their souls on edge. Who writes the play—the manager? This play mocks its author, unfolding as it pleases and according to the actors' abilities. It definitely depends on fate, which like the wind blows every which way. That's why the outcome is always a surprise to spectators and protagonists alike, except in cases of bribery or other inescapable tricks of destiny.

How many small theaters inhabit the great theater of soccer? How many stages fit inside that rectangle of green grass? Not all players perform with their legs alone. Some are masters in the art of tormenting their fellows. Wearing the mask of a saint incapable of harming a fly, such a player will spit at his opponent, insult him, push him, throw dirt in his eyes, give him a well-placed elbow to the chin, dig another into his ribs, pull his hair or his shirt, step on his foot when he stops or his hand when he's down—and all behind the referee's back and while the linesmen contemplate the passing clouds.

Some are wizards in the art of gaining advantage. Wearing the mask of a poor sad sack who looks like an imbecile but is really an idiot, such a player will take a penalty, a free kick, or a throw-in several leagues beyond the point indicated by the referee. And when he has to form a wall, he glides over to the spot very slowly, without lifting his feet, until the magic carpet deposits him right on top of the player about to kick the ball.

There are actors unsurpassed in the art of wasting time. Wearing the mask of a recently crucified martyr, such a player rolls in agony, clutching his knee or his head, and then lies prone on the grass. Minutes pass. At a snail's pace out comes the fat masseur, the holy hand, running with sweat, smelling of liniment, wearing a towel around his neck, and carrying a canteen in one hand and some infallible potion in the other. Hours go by, years go by, until the referee orders them to take that corpse off the field. And suddenly, whoosh, up jumps the player and the miracle of the resurrection occurs.

The Specialists

Before the match, the columnists formulate their disconcerting question: "Are you prepared to win?"

And they obtain an astonishing answer: "We will do everything possible to obtain victory."

Later on, the broadcasters take the floor. TV anchors know they can't compete with the images, so they keep them company. Radio commentators, on the other hand, are a less fainthearted breed. These masters of suspense do more running than the players and more skidding than the ball. With dizzying speed they describe a game that bears little resemblance to the one you are watching. In that waterfall of words the shot you see scraping the sky is grazing the crossbar, and the net where a spider placidly spins her web from post to post while the goalkeeper yawns faces an imminent goal.

When the vibrant day in the concrete colossus ends, the critics have their turn. Already they have interrupted the broadcast several times to tell the players what to do, but the players did not listen because they were too busy making mistakes. These ideologues of the WM formation against the MW, which is the same thing but backward, speak a language where scientific erudition alternates with war propaganda and lyrical ecstasy. And they always speak in the plural, because they are many.

The Language of Soccer Doctors

Let's sum up our point of view, formulating a first approximation of the tactical, technical, and physical problems of the contest waged this afternoon on the field of the Unidos Venceremos Soccer Club without turning to simplifications incompatible with this topic, which undoubtedly demands a more profound and detailed analysis, and without resorting to ambiguities which have been, are, and always will be alien to our lifelong dedication to serving the sporting public.

It would be easy for us to evade our responsibility and attribute the home team's setback to the restrained performance of its players, but the excessive sluggishness they undeniably demonstrated in today's match each time they received the ball in no way justifies, understand me well ladies and gentlemen, *in no way* justifies such a generalized and therefore unfair critique. No, no, and no. Conformity is not our style, as those of you who have followed us during the long years of our career well know, not only in our beloved country but also on the stage of international and even worldwide sport, wherever we have been called upon to fulfill our humble duty. So, as is our habit, we are going to pronounce all the syllables of every word: the organic potential of the game plan pursued by this struggling team has not been crowned with success simply and plainly because the team continues to be incapable of adequately channeling its expectations for greater offensive projection in the direction of the enemy goal. We said as much only this past Sunday and we affirm it today, with our head held high and without any hairs on our tongue, because we have always called a spade a spade and we will continue speaking the truth, though it hurts, fall who may, and no matter the cost.

⊛ ⊛ ⊛ ⊛ ⊛ ⊛ ⊛ ⊛ ⊛ ⊛ ⊛ ⊛ ⊛ ⊛

Choreographed War

In soccer, ritual sublimation of war, eleven men in shorts are the sword of the neighborhood, the city, or the nation. These warriors without weapons or armor exorcize the demons of the crowd and reaffirm its faith: in each confrontation between two sides, old hatreds and old loves passed from father to son enter into combat.

The stadium has towers and banners like a castle, as well as a deep and wide moat around the field. In the middle, a white line separates the territories in dispute. At each end stand the goals to be bombed with flying balls. The area directly in front of the goals is called the "danger zone."

In the center circle, the captains exchange pennants and shake hands as the ritual demands. The referee blows his whistle and the ball, another whistling wind, is set in motion. The ball travels back and forth, a player traps her and takes her for a ride until he gets pummeled in a tackle and falls spread-eagled. The victim does not rise. In the immensity of the green expanse, the player lies prostrate. From the immensity of the stands, voices thunder. The enemy crowd emits a friendly roar:

    "*¡Que se muera!*"
    "*Devi morire!*"
    "*Tuez-le!*"
    "*Mach ihn nieder!*"
    "*Let him die!*"
    "*Kill, kill, kill!*"

The Language of War

Utilizing a competent tactical variant of their planned strategy, our squad leaped to the charge, surprising the enemy unprepared. It was a brutal attack. When the home troops invaded enemy territory, our battering ram opened a breach in the most vulnerable flank of the defensive wall and infiltrated the danger zone. The artilleryman received the projectile and with a skillful maneuver got into shooting position, reared back for the kill, and brought the offensive to culmination with a cannonball that annihilated the guard. Then the defeated sentry, custodian of the seemingly unassailable bastion, fell to his knees with his face in his hands, while the executioner who shot him raised his arms to the cheering crowd.

The enemy did not retreat, but its stampedes never managed to sow panic in the home trenches, and time and again they crashed against our well-armored rear guard. Their men were shooting with wet powder, reduced to impotence by the gallantry of our gladiators, who battled like lions. When two of ours were knocked out of the fight, the crowd called in vain for the maximum sentence, but such atrocities fit for war and disrespectful of the gentlemanly rules of the noble sport of soccer continued with impunity.

At last, when the deaf and blind referee called an end to the contest, a well-deserved whistle discharged the defeated squad. Then the victorious throngs invaded the redoubt to hoist on their shoulders the eleven heroes of this epic gest, this grand feat, this great exploit that cost so much in blood, sweat, and tears. And our captain, wrapped in the standard of our fatherland that will never again be soiled by defeat, raised up the trophy and kissed the great silver cup. It was the kiss of glory!

The Stadium

Have you ever entered an empty stadium? Try it. Stand in the middle of the field and listen. There is nothing less empty than an empty stadium. There is nothing less mute than stands bereft of spectators.

At Wembley, shouts from the 1966 World Cup, which England won, still resound, and if you listen very closely you can hear groans from 1953 when England fell to the Hungarians. Montevideo's Centenario Stadium sighs with nostalgia for the glory days of Uruguayan soccer. Maracanã is still crying over Brazil's 1950 World Cup defeat. At Bombonera in Buenos Aires, drums boom from half a century ago. From the depths of Azteca Stadium, you can hear the ceremonial chants of the ancient Mexican ball game. The concrete terraces of Camp Nou in Barcelona speak Catalan, and the stands of San Mamés in Bilbao talk in Basque. In Milan, the ghost of Giuseppe Meazza scores goals that shake the stadium bearing his name. The final match of the 1974 World Cup, won by Germany, is played day after day and night after night at Munich's Olympic Stadium. King Fahd Stadium in Saudi Arabia has marble and gold boxes and carpeted stands, but it has no memory or much of anything to say.

The Ball

The Chinese used a ball made of leather and filled with hemp. In the time of the pharaohs the Egyptians used a ball made of straw or the husks of seeds, wrapped in colorful fabric. The Greeks and Romans used an ox bladder, inflated and sewn shut. Europeans of the Middle Ages and the Renaissance played with an oval-shaped ball filled with horsehair. In America the ball was made of rubber and bounced like nowhere else. The chroniclers of the Spanish Court tell how Hernán Cortés bounced a Mexican ball high in the air before the bulging eyes of Emperor Charles.

The rubber chamber, swollen with air and covered with leather, was born in the middle of the nineteenth century thanks to the genius of Charles Goodyear, an American from Connecticut. And long after that, thanks to the genius of Tossolini, Valbonesi, and Polo, three Argentines from Córdoba, the lace-free ball was born. They invented a chamber with a valve inflated by injection, and ever since the 1938 World Cup it has been possible to head the ball without getting hurt by the laces that once tied it together.

Until the middle of the twentieth century, the ball was brown. Then white. In our days it comes in different patterns of black on a white background. Now it has a waist of sixty centimeters and is dressed in polyurethane on polyethylene foam. Waterproof, it weighs less than a pound and travels more quickly than the old leather ball, which on rainy days barely moved.

They call it by many names: the sphere, the round, the tool, the globe, the balloon, the projectile. In Brazil no one doubts the ball is a woman. Brazilians call her pudgy, *gorduchinha*, or baby, *menina*, and they give her names like Maricota, Leonor, or Margarita.

Pelé kissed her in Maracaná when he scored his thousandth goal and Di Stéfano built her a monument in front of his house, a bronze ball with a plaque that says: *Thanks, old girl*.

She is loyal. In the final match of the 1930 World Cup, both teams insisted on playing with their own ball. Sage as Solomon, the referee decided that the first half would be played with the Argentine ball and the second with the Uruguayan ball. Argentina won the first half, and Uruguay the second. The ball can also be fickle, refusing to enter the goal because she changes her mind in midflight and curls away. You see, she is easily offended. She cannot stand getting kicked or hit out of spite. She insists on being caressed, kissed, lulled to sleep on the chest or the foot. She is proud, vain perhaps, and it is easy to understand why: she knows all too well that when she rises gracefully she brings joy to many a heart, and many a heart is crushed when she lands badly.

This Ming dynasty engraving is from the fifteenth century, but the ball could have been made by Adidas.

           23

Two historical images. The first is from a fragment of a mural painted over a thousand years ago in Tepantitla at Teotihuacán, Mexico: Hugo Sánchez's ancestor maneuvering the ball with his left. The second is a stylized drawing of a medieval relief from the cathedral at Gloucester, England.

The Origins

I n soccer, as in almost everything else, the Chinese were first. Five thousand years ago, Chinese jugglers had balls dancing on their feet, and it wasn't long before they organized the first matches. The net stood in the center of the field and the players had to keep the ball from touching the ground without using their hands. The sport continued from dynasty to dynasty, as can be seen on certain bas-relief monuments from long before Christ and in later Ming dynasty engravings, which show people playing with a ball that could have been made by Adidas.

We know that in ancient times the Egyptians and the Japanese had fun kicking a ball around. On the marble surface of a Greek tomb from five centuries before Christ a man is kneeing a ball. The plays of Antiphanes contain telling expressions like "long ball," "short pass," and "forward pass." They say that Julius Caesar was quick with his feet, and that Nero couldn't score. In any case, there is no doubt that while Jesus was dying on the cross the Romans were playing something fairly similar to soccer.

Roman legionaries kicked the ball all the way to the British Isles. Centuries later, in 1314, King Edward II stamped his seal on a royal decree condemning the game as plebeian and riotous: "Forasmuch as there is a great noise in the city caused by hustling over large balls, from which many evils may arise, which God forbid." Football, as it was already being called, left a slew of victims.

Matches were fought in gangs, and there were no limits on the number of players, the length of the match, or anything else. An entire town would play against another town, advancing with kicks and punches toward the goal, which at that time was a far-off windmill. The matches extended over several leagues and several days at the cost of several lives. Kings repeatedly outlawed these bloody events: In 1349, Edward III included soccer among games that were "stupid and utterly useless," and there were edicts against the sport signed by Henry IV in 1410 and Henry VI in 1447. The more it was banned, the more it was played, which only confirms that prohibition whets the appetite.

In 1592 in *The Comedy of Errors*, Shakespeare turned to soccer to formulate a character's complaint:

> *Am I so round with you as you with me,*
> *That like a football you do spurn me thus?*
> *You spurn me hence, and he will spurn me hither:*
> *If I last in this service, you must case me in leather.*

And a few years later in *King Lear*, the Earl of Kent taunted: "Nor tripped neither, you base football player!"

In Florence soccer was called *calcio*, as it is even now throughout Italy. Leonardo da Vinci was a fervent fan and Machiavelli loved to play. It was played in sides of twenty-seven men split into three lines, and they were allowed to use their hands and feet to hit the ball and gouge the bellies of their adversaries. Throngs of people attended the matches, which were held in the largest piazzas and on the frozen waters of the Arno. Far from Florence, in the gardens of the Vatican, popes Clement VII, Leo IX, and Urban VIII used to roll up their vestments to play *calcio*.

In Mexico and Central America a rubber ball filled in for the sun in a sacred ceremony performed as far back as 1500 BC. But we do not know when soccer began in many places of the Americas. The Indians of the Bolivian Amazon say they have been chasing a hefty rubber ball to put it between two posts without using their hands since time immemorial. In the eighteenth century, a Spanish priest from the Jesuit missions of the upper Paraná described an ancient custom of the Guaranís: "They do not throw the ball with their hands like us; rather, they propel it with the upper part of their bare foot." Among the Indians of Mexico and Central America, the ball was generally hit with the hip or the forearm, although paintings at Teotihuacán and Chichén-Itzá show the ball being kicked with the foot and the knee. A mural created over a thousand years ago in Tepantitla has an ancestor of Hugo Sánchez maneuvering the ball with his left. The match would end when the ball approached its destination: the sun arrived at dawn after traveling through the region of death. Then, for the sun to rise, blood would flow. According to some in the know, the Aztecs were in the habit of sacrificing the winners. Before cutting off their heads, they painted red stripes on their bodies. The chosen of the gods would offer their blood, so the earth would be fertile and the heavens generous.

The Rules of the Game

After centuries of official denial, the British Isles finally accepted the ball in its destiny. Under Queen Victoria soccer was embraced not only as a plebeian vice but as an aristocratic virtue.

The future leaders of society learned how to win by playing soccer in the courtyards of colleges and universities. There, upper-class brats unbosomed their youthful ardors, honed their discipline, tempered their anger, and sharpened their wits. At the other end of the social scale, workers had no need to test the limits of their bodies, since that is what factories and workshops were for, but the fatherland of industrial capitalism discovered that soccer, passion of the masses, offered entertainment and consolation to the poor and distraction from thoughts of strikes and other evils.

In its modern form, soccer comes from a gentleman's agreement signed by twelve English clubs in the autumn of 1863 in a London tavern. The clubs agreed to abide by rules established in 1848 at the University of Cambridge. In Cambridge soccer divorced rugby: carrying the ball with your hands was outlawed, although touching it was allowed, and kicking the adversary was also prohibited. "Kicks must be aimed only at the ball," warned one rule. A century and a half later some players still confuse the ball with their rival's skull owing to the similarity in shape.

The London accord put no limit on the number of players, or the size of the field, or the height of the goal, or the length of the contest. Matches lasted two or three hours and the protagonists chatted and smoked whenever the ball was flying in the distance. One modern rule was established: the offside. It was disloyal to score goals behind the adversary's back.

In those days no one played a particular position on the field. They all ran happily after the ball, each wherever he wanted, and everyone changed positions at will. It fell to Scotland around

1870 to organize teams with defense, midfielders, and strikers. By then sides had eleven players. From 1869 on, none of them could touch the ball with his hands, not even to catch and drop it to kick. In 1871 the exception to that taboo was born: the goal-keeper could use his entire body to defend the goal.

The goalkeeper protected a square redoubt narrower than to-day's and much taller. It consisted of two posts joined by a belt five and a half meters off the ground. The belt was replaced by a wooden crossbar in 1875. Goals were literally scored on the posts with a small notch. Today goals are registered on electronic score-boards, but the expression "to score a goal" has stuck. In some countries we call the goalmouth the *arco* and the one who defends it the *arquero*, even though it's all right angles and not an arch at all, perhaps because students at English colleges used courtyard arches for goals.

In 1872 the referee made his appearance. Until then, the play-ers were their own judges, and they themselves sanctioned any fouls committed. In 1880, chronometer in hand, the referee de-cided when the match was over and when anyone should be sent off, though he still ran things by shouting from the sidelines. In 1891 the referee stepped onto the playing field for the first time, blowing a whistle to call the first penalty kick in history and walk-ing twelve paces to indicate the spot where it was to be taken. For

⊚ ⊚ ⊚ ⊚ ⊚ ⊚ ⊚ ⊚ ⊚ ⊚ ⊚ ⊚ ⊚ ⊚ ⊚

some time the British press had been campaigning in favor of penalties because the players needed some protection in front of the goal, which was the scene of incredible butchery. A hair-raising list of players killed and bones broken had been published in the *Westminster Gazette*.

In 1882 English authorities allowed the throw-in. Eight years later the areas of the field were marked with lime and a circle was drawn at the center. That same year the goal gained a net to trap the ball and erase any doubts as to whether a goal had been scored.

After that the century died, and with it the British monopoly. In 1904 FIFA was born, the Fédération Internationale de Football Association, which has governed relations between ball and foot throughout the world ever since. Through all the world championships, few changes have been made to the British rules that first organized the sport.

The English Invasions

Outside a madhouse, in an empty lot in Buenos Aires, several blond boys were kicking a ball around.

"Who are they?" asked a child.

"Crazy people," answered his father. "Crazy English."

Journalist Juan José de Soiza Reilly remembers this from his childhood. At first, soccer seemed like a crazy man's game in the River Plate. But as the empire expanded, soccer became an export as typically British as Manchester cloth, railroads, loans from Barings, or the doctrine of free trade. It arrived on the feet of sailors who played by the dikes of Buenos Aires and Montevideo, while Her Majesty's ships unloaded blankets, boots, and flour, and took on wool, hides, and wheat to make more blankets, boots, and flour on the other side of the world. English citizens—diplomats, and managers of railroad and gas companies—formed the first local teams. The English of Montevideo and Buenos Aires staged Uruguay's first international competition in 1889, under a gigantic portrait of Queen Victoria, her eyes lowered in a mask of disdain. Another portrait of the queen of the seas watched over the first Brazilian soccer match in 1895, played between the British subjects of the Gas Company and the São Paulo Railway.

Old photographs show these pioneers in sepia tones. They were warriors trained for battle. Cotton and wool armor covered their entire bodies so as not to offend the ladies in attendance, who unfurled silk parasols and waved lace handkerchiefs. The only flesh the players exposed were their serious faces peering out from behind wax-twirled mustaches below caps or hats. Their feet were shod with heavy Mansfield shoes.

It did not take long for the contagion to spread. Sooner rather than later, the native-born gentlemen of local society started playing that crazy English game. From London they imported the shirts, shoes, thick ankle socks, and pants that reached from the chest to below the knee. Balls no longer confounded customs officers, who at first had not known how to classify the species. Ships also brought rulebooks to these far-off coasts of southern America, and with them came words that remained for many years to come: field, score, goal, goalkeeper, back, half, forward, out ball, penalty, offside. A "foul" merited punishment by the "referee," but the aggrieved player could accept an apology from the guilty party "as long as his apology was sincere and was expressed in proper English," according to the first soccer rulebook that circulated in the River Plate.

Meanwhile, other English words were being incorporated into the speech of Latin American countries in the Caribbean: pitcher, catcher, innings. Having fallen under US influence, these countries learned to hit a ball with a round wooden bat. The Marines shouldered bats next to their rifles when they imposed imperial order on the region by blood and by fire. Baseball became for the people of the Caribbean what soccer is for us.

Creole Soccer

The Argentine Football Association did not allow Spanish to be spoken at the meetings of its directors, and the Uruguay Association Football League outlawed Sunday matches because it was British custom to play on Saturday. But by the first years of the twentieth century, soccer was becoming a popular and local phenomenon on the shores of the River Plate. This sport, first imported to entertain the idle offspring of the well-to-do, had escaped its high window box, come to earth, and was setting down roots.

The process was unstoppable. Like the tango, soccer blossomed in the slums. It required no money and could be played with nothing more than sheer desire. In fields, in alleys, and on beaches, native-born kids and young immigrants played pickup using balls made of old socks filled with rags or paper and a couple of stones for a goal. Thanks to the language of soccer, which soon became universal, workers driven out of the countryside could communicate perfectly well with workers driven out of Europe. The Esperanto of the ball connected the native-born poor with peons who had crossed the sea from Vigo, Lisbon, Naples, Beirut, or Bessarabia with their dreams of building America—making a new world by laying bricks, carrying loads, baking bread, or sweeping streets. Soccer had made a lovely voyage: first

⊛ ⊛ ⊛ ⊛ ⊛ ⊛ ⊛ ⊛ ⊛ ⊛ ⊛ ⊛ ⊛ ⊛

organized in the colleges and universities of England, it brought
joy to the lives of South Americans who had never set foot in a
school.

On the playing fields of Buenos Aires and Montevideo, a style
came into being. A homegrown way of playing soccer, like the
homegrown way of dancing being invented in the *milonga* clubs.
Dancers drew filigrees on a single floor tile and soccer players created their own language in the tiny space where they chose to retain and possess the ball rather than kick it, as if their feet were
hands braiding the leather. On the feet of the first Creole virtu-
osos, *el toque,* the touch, was born: the ball was strummed as if it
were a guitar, a source of music.

At the same time, soccer was being tropicalized in Rio de
Janeiro and São Paulo by the poor who enriched it while they ap-
propriated it. No longer the possession of the few comfortable
youth who played by copying, this foreign sport became Brazilian, fertilized by the creative energies of the people discovering it.
And thus was born the most beautiful soccer in the world, made
of hip feints, undulations of the torso, and legs in flight, all of
which came from *capoeira,* the warrior dance of black slaves, and
from the joyful dance steps of the big-city slums.

As soccer became a popular passion and revealed its hidden
beauty, it disqualified itself as a dignified pastime. In 1915 the de-
mocratization of soccer drew complaints from the Rio de Janeiro
magazine *Sports*: "Those of us who have a certain position in society are obliged to play with workers, with drivers. . . . Playing this
sport is becoming an agony, a sacrifice, never a pastime."

The Story of Fla and Flu

The year 1912 saw the first classic in the history of Brazilian soccer: the first Fla–Flu. Fluminense beat Flamengo 3–2.

It was a stirring and violent match that caused numerous fainting spells among the spectators. The boxes were festooned with flowers, fruits, feathers, drooping ladies, and raucous gentlemen. While the gentlemen celebrated each goal by throwing their straw hats onto the playing field, the ladies let fall their fans and collapsed from the excitement of the goal or the oppression of heat and corset.

Flamengo had been born not long before, when Fluminense split after much saber rattling and many labor pains. Soon the father was sorry he had not strangled this smart aleck of a son in the cradle, but it was too late. Fluminense had spawned its own curse and nothing could be done.

From then on, father and son—rebellious son, abandoned father—dedicated their lives to hating each other. Each Fla–Flu classic is a new battle in a war without end. The two love the same city, lazy, sinful Rio de Janeiro, a city that languidly lets herself be loved, toying with both and surrendering to neither. Father and son play for the lover who plays with them. For her they battle, and she attends each duel dressed for a party.

The Opiate of the People?

How is soccer like God? Each inspires devotion among believers and distrust among intellectuals.

In 1902 in London, Rudyard Kipling made fun of soccer
and those who contented their souls with "the muddied oafs at
the goals." Three quarters of a century later in Buenos Aires, Jorge
Luis Borges was more subtle: he gave a lecture on the subject of
immortality on the same day and at the same hour that Argentina
was playing its first match in the 1978 World Cup.

The scorn of many conservative intellectuals comes from their
conviction that soccer worship is precisely the superstition people
deserve. Possessed by the ball, working stiffs think with their feet,
which is entirely appropriate, and fulfill their dreams in primitive
ecstasy. Animal instinct overtakes human reason, ignorance crushes
culture, and the riffraff get what they want.

In contrast, many leftist intellectuals denigrate soccer because it castrates the masses and derails their revolutionary ardor. Bread and circus, circus without the bread: hypnotized by the ball, which exercises a perverse fascination, workers forget who they are and let themselves be led about like sheep by their class enemies.

In the River Plate, once the English and the rich lost possession of the sport, the first popular clubs were organized in railroad workshops and shipyards. Several anarchist and socialist leaders denounced the clubs as a maneuver by the bourgeoisie to forestall strikes and disguise class divisions. The spread of soccer across the world was an imperialist trick to keep oppressed peoples trapped in an eternal childhood.

But the club Argentinos Juniors was born calling itself the Chicago Martyrs, in homage to those anarchist workers, and May 1 was the day chosen to launch the club Chacarita at a Buenos Aires anarchist library. In those first years of the twentieth century, plenty of left-leaning intellectuals celebrated soccer instead of repudiating it as a sedative of consciousness. Among them was the Italian Marxist Antonio Gramsci, who praised "this open-air kingdom of human loyalty."

A Rolling Flag

During the summer of 1916, in the midst of the World War, an English captain named Nevill launched an attack by kicking a ball. He leaped out from behind the parapet that had offered some cover and chased the ball toward the German trenches. His regiment, at first hesitant, followed. The captain was cut down by gunfire, but England conquered that no-man's-land and celebrated the battle as the first victory of British soccer on the front lines.

Many years later, toward the end of the century, the owner of Milan won the Italian elections with a chant from the stadiums, "Forza Italia!" Silvio Berlusconi promised to save Italy just the way he had saved Milan, the all-time champion superteam, and voters forgot that several of his companies were on the edge of ruin.

Soccer and fatherland are always connected, and politicians and dictators frequently exploit those links of identity. The Italian squad won the World Cups of 1934 and 1938 in the name of the fatherland and Mussolini, and the players started and finished each match by saluting the crowd with their right arms outstretched, giving three cheers for Italy.

For the Nazis too, soccer was a matter of state. A monument in the Ukraine commemorates the players of the 1942 Dynamo Kiev team. During the German occupation they committed the insane act of defeating Hitler's squad in the local stadium. Having been warned, "If you win, you die," they started out resigned to losing, trembling with fear and hunger, but in the end they could not contain their yearning for dignity. When the match was over, all eleven were shot with their club shirts on at the edge of a cliff.

Soccer and fatherland, fatherland and soccer: in 1934 while Bolivia and Paraguay were annihilating each other in the Chaco War, disputing a deserted corner of the map, the Paraguayan Red Cross formed a soccer team that played in several cities of Argentina and Uruguay and raised enough money to attend to the wounded of both sides.

Three years later, while General Franco, arm in arm with Hitler and Mussolini, bombed the Spanish Republic, a Basque team was on the road in Europe and the club Barcelona was playing in the United States and Mexico. The Basque government had sent the Euzkadi team to France and other countries to publicize their cause and raise funds for defense; Barcelona had sailed for America with the same mission. It was 1937 and Barcelona's captain had already fallen under Franco's bullets. On the soccer field and off, the two wandering teams embodied democracy under siege.

Only four of Barcelona's players made it back to Spain during the war. Of the Basques, only one. When the Republic was defeated, FIFA declared the exiled players to be in rebellion and threatened them with permanent suspension, but a few of them managed to find work with Latin American teams. Several of the

Basques formed the club España in Mexico, who were unbeatable in the early years. The Euzkadi center forward, Isidro Lángara, made his debut in Argentina in 1939. In his first match he scored four goals. That was for San Lorenzo, where Ángel Zubieta, who had played in Euzkadi's midfield, also starred. Later on, in Mexico, Lángara led the list of scorers in the 1945 championship.

The model club of Franco's Spain, Real Madrid, ruled the world between 1956 and 1960. This astonishing team won four Cups in a row in the Spanish League, five European Cups, and one Intercontinental. Real Madrid went everywhere and always left people with their mouths hanging open. The Franco dictatorship had found a traveling embassy that could not be beat. Goals broadcast by radio were more effective trumpets of triumph than the anthem "Cara al Sol." In 1959 one of the regime's political bosses, José Solís, voiced his gratitude to the players: "Thanks to you, people who used to hate us now understand us." Like El Cid, Real Madrid embodied all the virtues of Immortal Spain, even though its famous squad looked more like the Foreign Legion: the Frenchman Kopa, the Argentines Di Stéfano and Rial, the Uruguayan Santamaría, and the Hungarian Puskás.

Ferenc Puskás was called "Little Cannon Boom" for the smashing virtues of his left leg, which could also catch the ball like a glove. Other Hungarians, Lásló Kubala, Zoltán Czibor, and Sándor Kocsis, were stars with Barcelona in those years. In 1954 the cornerstone was laid for Camp Nou, the great Barcelona stadium built for Kubala. The old stadium could not hold the multitude that came to cheer his precision passes and deadly blasts. Czibor, meanwhile, struck sparks from his shoes. The other Hungarian on Barcelona, Kocsis, was a great header. "Head of Gold," they called him, and a sea of handkerchiefs celebrated his goals. They say Kocsis had the best head in Europe after Churchill.

Earlier on, in 1950, Kubala had formed a Hungarian team in exile, and that earned him a two-year suspension decreed by FIFA. It also suspended Puskás, Czibor, Kocsis, and other Hungarians for more than a year for playing on another exile team after Soviet tanks crushed the popular insurrection at the end of 1956.

In 1958 in the midst of its war of independence, Algeria formed a soccer team, which for the first time wore the national colors. Its line was made up of Rashid Makhloufi, Ben Tifour, and other Algerians who played professionally in France.

Blockaded by the colonial power, Algeria only managed to play against Morocco, which was kicked out of FIFA for several years for committing such a sin, and engage in several unimportant matches organized by sports unions in several Arab and Eastern European countries. FIFA slammed all the doors on the Algerian team, and the French soccer league blacklisted the players. Imprisoned by contracts, they were barred from ever returning to professional activity.

But after Algeria won its independence, the French had no alternative but to call up the players the fans longed for.

Blacks

In 1916 in the first South American championship, Uruguay creamed Chile 4–0. The next day, the Chilean delegation insisted the match be disallowed "because Uruguay had two Africans in the lineup." They were Isabelino Gradín and Juan Delgado. Gradín had scored two of the four goals.

Gradín was born in Montevideo, the great-grandson of slaves. He was a man who lifted people out of their seats when he erupted with astonishing speed, dominating the ball as easily as if he were walking. He would drive past the adversaries without a pause and score on the fly. He had a face like the holy host and was one of those guys who no one believes when they pretend to be bad.

Juan Delgado, also a great-grandson of slaves, was born in the town of Florida, in the Uruguayan countryside. Delgado liked to show off by dancing with a broom at Carnival and with the ball on the field. He talked while he played, and he liked to tease his opponents: "Pick me that bunch of grapes," he'd say as he sent the ball high. And as he shot he'd say to the keeper, "Jump for it, the sand is soft."

Back then Uruguay was the only country in the world with black players on its national team.

Zamora

He made his first-division debut when he was sixteen, still wearing short pants. Before taking the field with Espanyol of Barcelona, he put on a high-necked English jersey, gloves, and a hard cap like a helmet to protect himself from the sun and other blows. The year was 1917 and the attacks were like cavalry charges. Ricardo Zamora had chosen a perilous career. The only one in greater danger than the goalkeeper was the referee, known at that time as "The Nazarene," because the fields had no dugouts or fences to protect him from the vengeance of the fans. Each goal gave rise to a long hiatus while people ran onto the field either to embrace or throw punches.

Over the years the image of Zamora in those clothes became famous. He sowed panic among strikers. If they looked his way they were lost: with Zamora in the goal, the net would shrink and the posts would lose themselves in the distance.

They called him "The Divine One." For twenty years, he was the best goalkeeper in the world. He liked cognac and smoked three packs a day, plus the occasional cigar.

Illustrations from a soccer manual published in Barcelona at the beginning of the twentieth century.

Samitier

Like Zamora, Josep Samitier made his debut in the first division when he was sixteen. In 1918 he signed with Barcelona in exchange for a watch with a dial that glowed in the dark, something he had never seen, and a suit with a waistcoat.

It wasn't long before he was the team's ace and his life story was in kiosks all over the city. His name was on the lips of cabaret singers, bandied about on the stage, and revered in sports columns where they praised the "Mediterranean style" invented by Zamora and Samitier.

Samitier, a striker with a devastating shot, stood out for his cleverness, his domination of the ball, his utter lack of respect for the rules of logic, and his Olympian scorn for the boundaries of space and time.

Death on the Field

Abdón Porte, who wore the shirt of the Uruguayan club Nacional for more than two hundred matches over four years, always drew applause and sometimes cheers, until his lucky star fell.

They took him out of the starting lineup. He waited, asked to return, and did. But it was no use; the slump continued, the crowd whistled. On defense even tortoises got past him, on the attack he could not score a single goal.

At the end of the summer of 1918, in the Nacional stadium, Abdón Porte took his own life. He shot himself at midnight at the center of the field where he had been loved. All the lights were out. No one heard the gunshot.

They found him at dawn. In one hand he held a revolver, in the other a letter.

Friedenreich

In 1919 Brazil defeated Uruguay 1–0 and crowned itself champion of South America. People flooded the streets of Rio de Janeiro. Leading the celebration, raised aloft like a standard, was a muddy soccer boot with a little sign that proclaimed: "The glorious foot of Friedenreich." The next day that shoe, which had scored the winning goal, ended up in the display window of a downtown jewelry shop.

Artur Friedenreich, son of a German immigrant and a black washerwoman, played in the first division for twenty-six years and never earned a cent. No one scored more goals than he in the history of soccer, not even that other great Brazilian artilleryman, Pelé, who remains professional soccer's leading scorer. Friedenreich converted 1,329, Pelé 1,279.

This green-eyed mulatto founded the Brazilian style of play. He, or the devil who got into him through the soles of his feet, broke all the rules in the English manuals: to the solemn stadium of the whites Friedenreich brought the irreverence of brown boys who entertained themselves fighting over a rag ball in the slums. Thus was born a style open to fantasy, one that prefers pleasure to results. From Friedenreich onward, there have been no right angles in Brazilian soccer, just as there are none in the mountains of Rio de Janeiro or the buildings of Oscar Niemeyer.

From Mutilation to Splendor

I n 1921 the South American Cup was played in Buenos Aires. The president of Brazil, Epitácio Pessoa, issued a decree: for reasons of patriotic prestige there would be no brown skin on Brazil's national team. Of the three matches they played, the white team lost two.

Friedenreich did not play in that championship. Back then, to be black in Brazilian soccer was simply impossible, and being mulatto was a trial. Friedenreich always started late because it took him half an hour to iron his hair in the dressing room. The only mulatto player on Fluminense, Carlos Alberto, used to whiten his face with rice powder.

Later on, despite the owners of power, things began to change. With the passage of time, the old soccer mutilated by racism gave way to a soccer of multicolored splendor. After so many years it is obvious that Brazil's best players, from Friedenreich to Romário, by way of Domingos da Guia, Leônidas, Zizinho, Garrincha, Didi, and Pelé, have been blacks and mulattos. All of them came up from poverty, and some of them returned to it. By contrast, there have never been blacks or mulattos among Brazil's car-racing champions, which like tennis requires money.

In the global social pyramid, blacks are at the bottom and whites are at the top. In Brazil, where this is called "racial democracy," soccer is one of very few democratic venues where people of color can compete on an equal footing—up to a point. Even in soccer some are more equal than others. They all have the same rights, but the player who grew up hungry and the athlete who never missed a meal do not really compete on a level playing field. At least soccer offers a shot at social mobility for a poor child, usually black or mulatto, who had no other toy but a ball. The ball is the only fairy godmother he can believe in. Maybe she will feed him, maybe she will make him a hero, maybe even a god.

Misery trains him for soccer or for crime. From the moment of birth, that child is forced to turn his disadvantage into a weapon, and before long he learns to dribble around the rules of order that deny him a place. He learns the tricks of every trade and he becomes an expert in the art of pretending, surprising, breaking through where least expected, and throwing off an enemy with a hip feint or some other tune from the rascal's songbook.

The Second Discovery of America

For Pedro Arispe, homeland meant nothing. It was the place where he was born, which meant nothing to him because he had no choice in the matter. It was where he broke his back working as a peon in a packinghouse, and for him one boss was the same as any other no matter the country. But when Uruguay won the 1924 Olympics in France, Arispe was one of the winning players. While he watched the flag with the sun and four pale blue stripes rising slowly up the pole of honor, at the center of all the flags and higher than any other, Arispe felt his heart burst.

Four years later, Uruguay won gold again at the Olympics in the Netherlands. A prominent Uruguayan, Atilio Narancio, who in 1924 had mortgaged his house to pay for the players' passage, commented: "We are no longer just a tiny spot on the map of the world." The sky-blue shirt was proof of the existence of the nation: Uruguay was not a mistake. Soccer had pulled this tiny country out of the shadows of universal anonymity.

The authors of the miracles of '24 and '28 were workers and wanderers who got nothing from soccer but the pleasure of playing. Pedro Arispe was a meatpacker. José Nasazzi cut marble. "Perucho" Petrone was a grocer. Pedro Cea sold ice. José Leandro Andrade was a carnival musician and bootblack. They were all twenty years old or a little older, though in the pictures they look like old men. They cured their wounds with salt water, vinegar plasters, and a few glasses of wine.

In 1924 they arrived in Europe in third-class steerage and then traveled on borrowed money in second-class carriages, sleeping on wooden benches and playing match after match in exchange for room and board. Before the Paris Olympics, they played nine matches in Spain and won all nine of them.

It was the first time that a Latin American team had played in Europe. Their first Olympic match was against Yugoslavia. The Yugoslavs sent spies to the practice session. The Uruguayans caught on and practiced by kicking the ground and sending the ball up into the clouds, tripping at every step and crashing into each other. The spies reported: "It makes you feel sorry, these poor boys came from so far away."

Barely two thousand fans showed up. The Uruguayan flag was flown upside down, the sun on its head, and instead of the national anthem they played a Brazilian march. That afternoon, Uruguay defeated Yugoslavia 7–0.

And then something like the second discovery of America occurred. Match after match, crowds lined up to see those men, slippery like squirrels, who played chess with the ball. The English squad had perfected the long pass and the high ball, but these disinherited children, begotten in far-off America, did not walk in their fathers' footsteps. They chose to invent a game of close passes directly to the foot, with lightning changes in rhythm and high-speed dribbling. Henri de Montherlant, an aristocratic writer, published his enthusiasm: "A revelation! Here we have real soccer. Compared with this, what we knew before, what we played, was no more than a schoolboy's hobby."

Uruguay's success at the '24 and '28 Olympics, and its subsequent World Cup victories in 1930 and 1950, owed a large debt to the government's policy of building sports fields around the country to promote physical education. Now, years later, all that remains of the state's social calling, and of that great soccer, is nostalgia. Several players, like the very subtle Enzo Francescoli, have managed to inherit and renovate the old arts, but in general Uruguayan soccer is a far cry from what it used to be. Ever fewer children play it and ever fewer men play it gracefully. Nevertheless, there is no Uruguayan who does not consider himself a PhD in tactics and strategy, and a scholar of soccer history. Uruguayans' passion for soccer comes from those days long ago, and its deep roots are still alive. Every time the national team plays, no matter against whom, the country holds its breath. Politicians, singers, and carnival barkers shut their mouths, lovers suspend their caresses, and flies refuse to budge.

Andrade

Europe had never seen a black man play soccer.

In the 1924 Olympics, the Uruguayan José Leandro Andrade dazzled everyone with his exquisite moves. A midfielder, this rubber-bodied giant would sweep the ball downfield without ever touching an adversary, and when he launched the attack he would brandish his body and send them all scattering. In one match he crossed half the field with the ball sitting on his head. The crowds cheered him, the French press called him "The Black Marvel."

When the tournament was over, Andrade spent some time hanging around Paris as errant Bohemian and king of the cabarets. Patent leather shoes replaced his whiskery hemp sandals from Montevideo and a top hat took the place of his worn cap. Newspaper columns of the time praised the figure of that monarch of the Pigalle night: jaunty step, oversized grin, half-closed eyes always staring into the distance. And dressed to kill: silk handkerchief, striped jacket, bright yellow gloves, and a cane with a silver handle.

Andrade died in Montevideo many years later. His friends had planned several benefits for him, but none of them ever came off. He died of tuberculosis, in utter poverty.

He was black, South American, and poor, the first international idol of soccer.

Ringlets

They called the successive figure eights Uruguayan players drew on the field *moñas*, ringlets. French journalists wanted the secret of that witchcraft that cast rival players in stone. Through an interpreter, José Leandro Andrade revealed the formula: the players trained by chasing chickens that fled making S's on the ground. Journalists believed it and published the story.

Decades later, good ringlets were still cheered as loudly as goals in South American soccer. My childhood memory is filled with them. I close my eyes and I see, for example, Walter Gómez, that dizzying bushwhacker who would dive into the swamp of enemy legs with ringlet after ringlet and leave a wake of fallen bodies. The stands would confess:

> *We'd all rather fast*
> *than miss a Walter Gómez pass.*

He liked to knead the ball, retain it and caress it; if it got away from him, he would feel insulted. No coach would dare tell him, as they say now: "If you want to knead, go work in a bakery."

The ringlet was not just a bit of tolerated mischief, it was a joy the crowd demanded. Today such works of art are outlawed, or at least viewed with grave suspicion, and are considered selfish exhibitionism, a betrayal of team spirit, and utterly useless against the iron defensive systems of modern soccer.

The Olympic Goal

When the Uruguayan team returned from the 1924 Olympics, the Argentines challenged them to a friendly match in Buenos Aires. Uruguay lost by one goal.

Left wing Cesáreo Onzari was the author of the winning goal. He took a corner and the ball went directly into the net without anyone else touching it. He was the first in soccer history to score a goal that way. The Uruguayans were left speechless. When they found their tongues, they protested. They claimed the goalkeeper, Mazali, was pushed when the ball was in the air. The referee wouldn't listen. Then they howled that Onzari hadn't intended to shoot at the net and that the goal had been scored by the wind.

In homage or in irony, that rarity became known in South America as the "Olympic goal." It is still called that, on the rare occasions it occurs. Onzari spent the rest of his life swearing it wasn't by chance. And though years have gone by, the mistrust continues: every time a corner kick shakes the net without intermediaries, the crowd celebrates the goal with an ovation, but doesn't quite believe it.

Goal by Piendibene

It was 1926. The scorer, José Piendibene, did not celebrate. Piendibene, a man of rare mastery and rarer modesty, never celebrated his goals, so as not to offend.

The Uruguayan club Peñarol was playing in Montevideo against Espanyol of Barcelona, and they couldn't find a way to penetrate the goal defended by Zamora. The play came from behind. Anselmo slipped around two adversaries, sent the ball across to Suffiati, and then took off expecting a pass back. But Piendibene asked for it. He caught the pass, eluded Urquizú, and closed in on the goal. Zamora saw that Piendibene was shooting for the right corner and he leaped to block it. The ball hadn't moved; she was asleep on his foot. Piendibene tossed her softly to the left side of the empty net. Zamora managed to jump back, a cat's leap, and he grazed the ball with his fingertips when it was already too late.

The Bicycle Kick

Ramón Unzaga invented the move on the field at the Chilean port of Talcahuana: body in the air, back to the ground, he shot the ball backward with a sudden snap of his legs, like the blades of scissors.

It was some years later when this acrobatic act came to be called the *chilena*. In 1927, when club Colo-Colo traveled to Europe and striker David Arellano performed it in the stadiums of Spain, Spanish journalists cheered the splendor of this unknown gambol, and they baptized it *chilena* because, like strawberries and the cueca, it had come from Chile.

After several flying goals Arellano died that year, in the stadium at Valladolid, killed in a fatal encounter with a fullback.

Scarone

Forty years before the Brazilians Pelé and Coutinho, the Uruguayans Scarone and Cea rolled over the rivals' defense with passes from the thigh and zigzags that sent the ball back and forth from one to the other all the way to the goal, yours and mine, close and right to the foot, question and answer, call and response. The ball rebounded without a moment's pause, as if off a wall. That's what they called the River Plate style of attack back in those days: "The Wall."

Héctor Scarone served up passes like offerings and scored goals with a marksmanship he sharpened during practice sessions by knocking over bottles at thirty meters. And though he was rather short, when it came to jumping he was up long before the rest. Scarone knew how to float in the air, violating the law of gravity. He would leap for the ball, break free of his adversaries, and spin around to face the goal. Then, still aloft, he would head it in.

They called him "The Magician" because he pulled goals out of a hat, and they also called him "The Gardel of Soccer" because while he played he sang like no one else.

Goal by Scarone

It was 1928, during the Olympic final.

Uruguay and Argentina were tied when Píriz fired the ball across to Tarasconi and advanced toward the penalty area. Borjas met the ball with his back to the goal and headed it to Scarone, screaming, "Yours, Héctor!" and Scarone kicked it sharply on the fly. The Argentine goalkeeper, Bossio, dove for it but it had already hit the net. The ball bounced defiantly back onto the field. Uruguayan striker Figueroa sent it in again, punishing the ball with a swift kick, because leaving the goal like that was bad form.

The Occult Forces

A Uruguayan player, Adhemar Canavessi, sacrificed himself to avert the damage his presence would have caused in the final match of the 1928 Olympics in Amsterdam. Uruguay was to play Argentina. Every time Canavessi had faced the Argentines, Uruguay had lost, and the last time he had the bad luck to score a goal against his own side. So he got off the bus taking the players to the stadium. In Amsterdam, without Canavessi, Uruguay won.

The previous day, Carlos Gardel had sung for the Argentine players at the hotel where they were staying. To bring them luck, he had brought out a new tango called "Dandy." Two years later, just before the final of the 1930 World Cup, it happened again: Gardel sang "Dandy" to wish the team success and Uruguay won the final. Many swear his intentions were beyond reproach, but there are those who believe therein lies the proof that Gardel was Uruguayan.

Goal by Nolo

It was 1929. Argentina was playing Paraguay.

Nolo Ferreira brought the ball up from right at the back. He broke open a path, leaving a string of fallen bodies, until he suddenly found himself face-to-face with the entire defense lined up in a wall. Then Nolo stopped. He stood there passing the ball from one foot to the other, from one instep to the other, not letting it touch the ground. His adversaries tilted their heads from left to right and right to left, in unison, hypnotized, their gaze fixed on that pendulum of a ball. The back-and-forth went on for centuries, until Nolo found a hole and shot without warning: the ball pierced the wall and shook the net.

The mounted police got off their horses to congratulate him. Twenty thousand people were on the field, but every Argentine will swear he was there.

❀ ❀ ❀ ❀ ❀ ❀ ❀ ❀ ❀ ❀ ❀ ❀ ❀ ❀

The 1930 World Cup

An earthquake was shaking the south of Italy and burying 1,500 Neapolitans, Marlene Dietrich was singing "Falling in Love Again." Stalin was completing his usurpation of the Russian Revolution, and the poet Vladimir Mayakovsky was committing suicide. The English were jailing Mahatma Gandhi, who by demanding independence and loving his country had brought India to a standstill. Under the same banner in the other Indies, our Indies, Augusto César Sandino was rousing the peasants of Nicaragua and US Marines were burning the crops to defeat him by hunger.

In the United States some were dancing to the new boogie-woogie, but the euphoria of the Roaring Twenties had been knocked out cold by ferocious blows from the crash of '29. When the New York Stock Exchange tanked, it devastated international commodity prices and dragged several Latin American governments into the abyss. The price of tin took a nosedive off the precipice of the global crisis, pulling Bolivian President Hernando Siles after it and putting a general in his place, while the collapse of meat and wheat prices finished President Hipólito Yrigoyen in Argentina and installed another general in his place. In the Dominican Republic, the fall in sugar prices opened the long cycle of dictatorship of also-general Rafael Leónidas Trujillo, who was inaugurating his regime by baptizing the capital city and the port with his own name.

In Uruguay, the coup d'état was not to strike until three years later. In 1930 the country had eyes and ears only for the first World Cup. Uruguayan victories in the previous two Olympics held in Europe made the country the obvious choice to host the tournament.

Twelve nations arrived at the port of Montevideo. All Europe was invited, but only four teams crossed the ocean to these southern shores. "That's far away from everything," Europeans said, "and the passage is expensive."

A ship brought the Jules Rimet trophy from France, accompanied by FIFA president Monsieur Jules himself and by the reluctant French team.

With pomp and circumstance Uruguay inaugurated the monumental showcase it had taken eight months to build. The stadium was called Centenario to celebrate the constitution, which a century before had denied civil rights to women, the illiterate, and the poor. In the stands not a pin would have fit when Uruguay and Argentina faced each other in the final. The stadium was a sea of felt hats and canopies over cameras with tripods. The goalkeepers wore caps and the referee black plus fours.

The final of the 1930 World Cup did not merit more than a twenty-line column in the Italian daily *La Gazzetta dello Sport*. After all, it was a repeat of the Amsterdam Olympics in 1928: the two nations of the River Plate insulted Europe by showing the world where the best soccer was played. As in '28, Argentina took second place. Uruguay, losing 2–1 at the half, ended up winning 4–2 and was crowned champion. To referee the final, the Belgian John Langenus demanded life insurance, but nothing more serious occurred than a few tussles in the stands. Afterward, in Buenos Aires, a crowd stoned the Uruguayan consulate.

⊛ ⊛ ⊛ ⊛ ⊛ ⊛ ⊛ ⊛ ⊛ ⊛ ⊛ ⊛ ⊛ ⊛ ⊛ ⊛

Third place went to the United States, which had among its players several recent Scottish immigrants, and fourth place went to Yugoslavia.

Not a single match ended in a draw. The Argentine Stábile headed up the list of scorers with eight goals, followed by the Uruguayan Cea with five. Louis Laurent of France scored the first goal in World Cup history, against Mexico.

Nasazzi

Not even X rays could get through him. They called him "The Terrible."

"The field is a jar," he liked to say. "And the mouth of the jar is the penalty area."

There, in the box, he was boss.

José Nasazzi, captain of the Uruguayan teams of '24, '28, and '30, was the first caudillo of Uruguayan soccer. He was the windmill of the entire team, which worked to the rhythm of his shouts of warning, disappointment, and encouragement. No one ever heard him complain.

Camus

In 1930 Albert Camus was Saint Peter guarding the gate for the University of Algiers soccer team. He had been playing goalkeeper since childhood, because in that position your shoes don't wear out as fast. Son of a poor home, Camus could not afford the luxury of running the fields; every night, his grandmother examined the soles of his shoes and gave him a beating if she found them worn.

During his years in the net, Camus learned many things: "I learned that the ball never comes where you expect it to. That helped me a lot in life, especially in large cities where people don't tend to be what they claim."

He also learned to win without feeling like God and to lose without feeling like rubbish, skills not easily acquired, and he learned to unravel several mysteries of the human soul, whose labyrinths he explored later on in a dangerous journey on the page.

Juggernauts

One of the world champion Uruguayans, "Perucho" Petrone, packed up and moved to Italy. The afternoon in 1931 when Petrone made his debut for Fiorentina, he scored eleven goals.

He did not last long there. He was the top scorer in the Italian championship and Fiorentina offered him everything, but Petrone tired quickly of the hurrahs of fascism on the rise. Fed up and homesick, he went back to Montevideo where for a while he continued scoring his scorched-earth goals. He wasn't yet thirty when he had to leave soccer for good. FIFA forced him out because he broke his contract with Fiorentina.

They say Petrone's shot could knock down a wall. Who knows? One thing is for sure: it knocked out goalkeepers and broke through nets.

Meanwhile, on the other shore of the River Plate, the Argentine Bernabé Ferreyra was also shooting cannonballs with the fury of the possessed. Fans from every team went to see "The Wild Animal" start out deep, cut his way through the defense, and put the ball in the net and the keeper along with it.

Before and after each match and at halftime as well, they would play a tango over the loudspeakers composed in homage to Bernabé's artillery barrages. In 1932 the newspaper *Crítica* offered a sizable prize to the goalkeeper who could stop him from scoring. One afternoon that year, Bernabé had to take off his shoes for a group of journalists to prove no iron bars were hidden in the toes.

Turning Pro

Even though recent scandals ("clean hands, clean feet") have put the bosses of Italy's biggest clubs on the spot, soccer is still among the country's ten most important industries, and it remains a magnet for South American players.

Italy was already a Mecca way back in the time of Mussolini. Nowhere else in the world did they pay so well. Players would threaten the owners with "I'm going to Italy," and those magic words would loosen the purse strings. Some really did go, traveling by ship from Buenos Aires, Montevideo, São Paulo, and Rio de Janeiro, and if they didn't have Italian parents or grandparents somebody in Rome would invent a family on the spot for immediate citizenship.

The exodus of players was one factor that led to the birth of professional soccer in our countries. In 1931 Argentina turned pro, and Uruguay followed suit the next year. In Brazil a professional league was launched in 1934. That was when they legalized payments previously made under the table, and the player became a worker. The contract tied him to the club full-time and for life, and he could not change his workplace unless the team sold him. Like a factory worker, the player traded his labor for a wage and became as much a prisoner on the field as a serf on a manor. But in the early days the demands of professional soccer weren't great: only two hours a week of obligatory training. In Argentina anyone missing a practice session without a doctor's note paid a five-peso fine.

The 1934 World Cup

Johnny Weissmuller was doing his first Tarzan howl, the first mass-produced deodorant was hitting the market, and Louisiana police were shooting down Bonnie and Clyde. Bolivia and Paraguay, the two poorest countries in South America, were fighting in the name of Standard Oil and Shell and bleeding over oil in the Chaco. Sandino, having defeated the Marines in Nicaragua, was being shot dead in an ambush and Somoza, the murderer, was inaugurating his dynasty. In China, Mao was beginning his Long March. In Germany, Hitler was being crowned *Führer* of the Third Reich and was promulgating laws to defend the Aryan race, which forced sterilization on criminals and on anyone with a hereditary disease, while in Italy Mussolini was inaugurating the second World Cup.

Posters for the championship showed Hercules balancing a ball on his foot while doing the fascist salute. For Il Duce the 1934 World Cup in Rome was an elaborate propaganda operation. Mussolini attended every match, sitting in the box of honor, his chin raised toward stands filled with black shirts. The eleven players of the Italian squad dedicated their victories to him, their right arms outstretched.

But the road to the title was not easy. The second-round match between Italy and Spain turned out to be the most grueling in the history of World Cup play. The battle lasted 210 minutes and did not end until the following day, by which time war wounds or sheer exhaustion had sidelined several players. Italy won but finished without four of its starting players, Spain without seven. Among the injured Spaniards were the two best players: the striker Lángara and the keeper Zamora, who hypnotized anyone who set foot in the box.

Italy waged the final against Czechoslovakia in National Fascist Party Stadium and won 2–1. Two Argentines recently nationalized as Italians did their part: Orsi scored the first goal, dribbling around the goalkeeper, and the other Argentine, Guaita, made a pass to Schiavio to set up the goal that gave Italy its first World Cup.

In 1934 sixteen countries participated: twelve from Europe and three from Latin America, plus Egypt, the lone representative of the rest of the world. The reigning champion, Uruguay, refused because Italy had not come to the first World Cup in Montevideo.

Germany and Austria came in third and fourth. The Czech Nejedly was the leading scorer with five goals, followed by Conen from Germany and Schiavio from Italy with four apiece.

God and the Devil in Rio de Janeiro

One very rainy night while the year 1937 was dying, an enemy fan buried a toad in Vasco da Gama's playing field and called down a curse: "Vasco won't win a championship for the next twelve years! They won't, if there is a God in heaven!" He was a fan of a humble team that Vasco da Gama had beaten 12–0; Arubinha was his name.

For years, fans and players alike searched for that toad on and around the field. They never found it. The playing field was so pockmarked, it looked like a moonscape. Vasco da Gama hired the best players in Brazil, put together sides that were veritable powerhouses, but they kept on losing.

At last in 1945, the team won the Rio trophy and broke the curse. They had not been champions since 1934. Eleven years of drought. "God gave us a little discount," the club president commented.

Much later, in 1953, the team with problems was Flamengo, the most popular club not only in Rio de Janeiro but in all Brazil, the only one that is the home team wherever it plays. Their fans, who are the most numerous and fervent in the world, were dying of hunger. Then a Catholic priest, one Father Goes, offered a guarantee of victory as long as the players attended his mass before each match and said the rosary kneeling before the altar.

Flamengo won the championship three years in a row. Their rivals protested to Cardinal Jaime Câmara: Flamengo was using outlawed weapons. Father Goes defended himself claiming all he did was show them the way of the Lord. The players continued saying their rosaries of black and red beads, colors that are not only Flamengo's but also those of an African deity who incarnates Jesus and Satan at the same time. The fourth year Flamengo lost the championship. The players stopped going to mass and never said the rosary again. Father Goes asked the pope in Rome for help, but he never answered.

Father Romualdo, on the other hand, obtained the pope's permission to become a partner in Fluminense. The priest attended every practice session. The players did not like it one bit. Twelve years had passed since Fluminense had last won the Rio trophy, and it was bad luck to have that big black bird standing at the edge of the field. The players shouted insults at him, unaware that Father Romualdo had been deaf since birth.

One fine day, Fluminense started to win. They won one championship, then another and another. Now the players would only practice in the shadow of Father Romualdo. After every goal they kissed his cassock. On weekends the priest watched the matches from the box of honor and babbled who knows what against the referee and the opposing players.

The Sources of Misfortune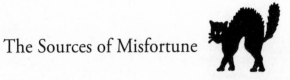

Everyone knows it is bad luck to step on a toad or on the shadow of a tree, to walk under a ladder, to sit or sleep backward, to open an umbrella indoors, to count your teeth, or break a mirror. But in soccer that barely scratches the surface.

Carlos Bilardo, coach of the Argentine team for the World Cups in 1986 and 1990, did not let his players eat chicken because it would give them bad luck. He made them eat beef, which gave them uric acid instead.

Silvio Berlusconi, owner of Milan, forbade fans from singing the club's anthem, the traditional chant "Milan, Milan," because its malevolent vibrations paralyzed his players' legs; in 1987 he commissioned a new anthem, "Milan Nei Nostri Cuori."

Freddy Rincón, Colombia's black giant, disappointed his many admirers at the '94 World Cup. He played without a drop of enthusiasm. Afterward we learned that it wasn't from a lack of desire, but an excess of fear. A prophet from Buenaventura, Rincón's home on the Colombian coast, had foretold the results of the championship, which turned out exactly as predicted, and warned that he would break his leg if he was not very careful. "Watch out for the girl with freckles," he said, referring to the ball, "and for the one with hepatitis, and the one covered in blood," alluding to the yellow and red cards of the referee.

On the eve of that Cup's final, Italian specialists in the occult declared their country would win. "Numerous evil spirits from black magic will defeat Brazil," the Italian Magicians Association assured the press. The contrary result did not add to the prestige of the profession.

Amulets and Spells

Many players put their right foot first and cross themselves when they step onto the field. Some go directly to the empty goal and kick one in or kiss the posts. Others touch the grass and bring their fingers to their lips.

Often you see a player wearing a little medal around his neck or a magic band tied around his wrist. If his penalty kick goes awry, it's because someone spat on the ball. If he misses an easy shot, it's because some witch closed the enemy goal. If he loses the match, it's because he gave away his shirt after the last victory.

Amadeo Carrizo, goalkeeper for the Argentine club River Plate, went eight matches with his net untouched thanks to the powers of a cap he wore day and night. That cap exorcised the demons of the goal. One afternoon Ángel Clemente Rojas, a player for Boca Juniors, stole it. Without his amulet, Carrizo let two goals by and River lost the match.

A leading Spanish player, Pablo Hernández Coronado, says that when Real Madrid refurbished its stadium the team went six years without winning a championship, until a fan broke the curse by burying a head of garlic in the center of the playing field. Barcelona's celebrated forward Luis Suárez did not believe in curses, but he knew that every time he knocked over a glass of wine while eating he was going to score a few goals.

To invoke the evil spirits of defeat, fans throw salt on the enemy's field. To scare them off, they sow their own field with fistfuls of wheat or rice. Others light candles, offer the earth cane liquor, or toss flowers into the sea. Some fans seek protection by praying to Jesus of Nazareth and the blessed souls who died by fire, drowning, or losing their way. In several places Saint George's lances and those of his African twin, Ogum, have proved very effective against the dragon of the evil eye.

Thoughtful gestures are appreciated. Fans favored by the gods crawl on their knees up steep slopes, wrapped in the team flag, or they spend the rest of their days whispering the million rosaries they swore to say. When Botafogo was crowned champion in 1957, Didi left the field without going to the dressing room and, still in his uniform, fulfilled the promise he had made to his patron saint: he walked across the city of Rio de Janeiro from end to end.

But deities do not always have time to come to the aid of soccer players tormented by misfortune. The Mexican team arrived at the 1930 World Cup overwhelmed by pessimistic predictions. Just before the match against France, Mexican coach Juan Luque de Serrallonga gave the players a pep talk at his hotel in Montevideo. He assured them that the Virgin of Guadalupe was praying for them back home on Tepeyac Hill.

The coach was not apprised of the Virgin's busy schedule. France scored four goals and Mexico finished in last place.

Erico

During the Chaco War, while the peasants of Bolivia and Paraguay were marching to slaughter, Paraguay's soccer players were in other countries playing to raise money for the many who fell helplessly wounded in a desert where no birds sang and people left no footprints. That's how Arsenio Erico came to Buenos Aires, and in Buenos Aires he stayed. Argentina's leading scorer of all time was Paraguayan. Erico scored over forty goals a season.

That magician had secret springs hidden in his body. He could jump without bending his knees, and his head always reached higher than the goalkeeper's hands. The more relaxed his legs seemed, the more powerfully they would explode to lash out at the goal. Often Erico would whip it in with his heel. There was no deadlier backheel in the history of soccer.

When Erico wasn't scoring goals, he was offering them on a platter to his teammates. Cátulo Castillo dedicated a tango to him:

> Your pass from the heel or head is such
> a marvelous feat
> a thousand years won't see a repeat.

And he did it with the elegance of a dancer. "He's Nijinski," commented the French writer Paul Morand, when he saw him play.

The 1938 World Cup

M ax Theiler was discovering a vaccine for yellow fever, color photography was being born, Walt Disney was launching *Snow White*, and Eisenstein was filming *Alexander Nevsky*. Nylon, invented not long before by a Harvard professor, was being turned into parachutes and ladies' stockings.

The Argentine poets Alfonsina Storni and Leopoldo Lugones were killing themselves. Lázaro Cárdenas was nationalizing Mexico's oil and confronting a blockade and other Western furies. Orson Welles was broadcasting a Martian invasion of the United States to frighten the gullible, while Standard Oil was demanding a real invasion of Mexico to punish the heresy of Cárdenas and put an end to his bad example.

In Italy *Manifesto on Race* was being written and anti-Semitic attacks were on the rise. Germany was occupying Austria; Hitler was hunting down Jews and devouring territory. The English government was ordering people to stockpile food and teaching them to defend themselves against poison gas. Franco was cornering the last bastions of the Spanish Republic and receiving the recognition of the Vatican. César Vallejo was dying in Paris, probably in the pouring rain, while Sartre was publishing *Nausea*. And there, in Paris, under the darkening shadows of the war to come, where Picasso's *Guernica* was on display to denounce the time of infamy, the third World Cup was getting under way. In Colombes stadium, French president Albert Lebrun made the ceremonial kickoff: he aimed at the ball but cuffed the ground.

As with the previous Cup, this was a European championship.
Only two South American countries joined eleven from Europe.
A team from Indonesia, still called the Dutch East Indies, came to
Paris as the sole representative of the rest of the planet.

Germany's side incorporated five players from recently an-
nexed Austria. Thus reinforced, with swastikas on their chests and
all the Nazi symbols of power at hand, the German squad came
on strong, claiming invincibility, only to trip and fall to modest
Switzerland. The German defeat occurred a few days before Aryan
supremacy suffered another rude blow in New York, when black
boxer Joe Louis pulverized German champion Max Schmeling.

Italy, on the other hand, pulled off a repeat of the previous
World Cup contest. In the semifinal, the Azzurri defeated Brazil.
One penalty was questionable, but Brazil protested in vain. As in
'34, all the referees were European.

Then came the final: Italy against Hungary. For Mussolini,
winning was a matter of state. On the eve of the match, the Italian
players received a three-word telegram from Rome, signed by the
Fascist leader: "Win or die." They did not have to die because

Italy won 4–2. The following day the victors wore military uniforms to the closing ceremony, presided over by Il Duce.

The daily *La Gazzetta dello Sport* exalted "the apotheosis of Fascist sports symbolized by this victory of the race." Not long before, the official press had celebrated Italy's defeat of Brazil with these words: "We salute the triumph of Italic intelligence over the brute force of the Negroes."

But it was the international press that chose the best players of the tournament, among them two black men, Brazilians Leônidas and Domingos da Guia. With seven goals Leônidas was the leading scorer, followed by the Hungarian Zsengellér with six. The most beautiful goal scored by Leônidas came against Poland. Playing in a torrential storm, he lost his shoe in the mud of the penalty area and made the goal barefoot.

Goal by Meazza

It was at the 1938 World Cup. In the semifinal, Italy and Brazil were risking their necks for all or nothing.

Italian striker Piola suddenly collapsed as if he'd been shot, and with the last flutter of life in his finger he pointed at Brazilian defender Domingos da Guia. The referee believed him and blew his whistle: penalty. While the Brazilians screamed to high heaven and Piola got up and dusted himself off, Giuseppe Meazza placed the ball on the firing point.

Meazza was the dandy of the picture. A short, handsome Latin lover and an elegant artilleryman of penalties, he lifted his chin to the goalkeeper like a matador before the final charge. His feet, as soft and knowing as hands, never missed. But Walter, the Brazilian keeper, was good at blocking penalty kicks and felt confident.

Meazza began his run-up and, just when he was about to execute the kick, he dropped his shorts. The crowd was stupefied and the referee nearly swallowed his whistle. But Meazza, never pausing, grabbed his pants with one hand and sent the goalkeeper, disarmed by laughter, down to defeat.

That was the goal that put Italy in the final.

Leônidas

He had the dimensions, speed, and cunning of a mosquito. At the '38 World Cup a journalist from *Paris Match* counted six legs on him and suggested black magic was responsible. I don't know if the journalist noticed, but Leônidas's many legs had the diabolical ability to grow several yards and fold over or tie themselves in knots.

Leônidas da Silva stepped onto the field the day Brazilian great Arthur Friedenreich, already in his forties, retired. Leônidas received the scepter from the old master. It wasn't long before they named a brand of cigarettes and a candy bar after him. He got more fan letters than a movie star; the letters asked him for a picture, an autograph, or a government job.

Leônidas scored many goals but never counted them. A few were made from the air, his feet twirling, upside down, back to the goal. He was skilled in the acrobatics of the *chilena*, which Brazilians call the "bicycle."

Leônidas's goals were so pretty that even the goalkeeper would get up and congratulate him.

Domingos

To the east, the Great Wall of China. To the west, Domingos da Guia.

In the entire history of soccer no fullback was more solid. Domingos was champion in four cities—Rio de Janeiro, São Paulo, Montevideo, and Buenos Aires—and he was adored by all four. When he played, the stadiums were always jam-packed.

Fullbacks used to stick like stamps to the attacking strikers and peel off the ball as quickly as possible, wafting it to high heaven before it burned their feet. Domingos, in contrast, let his adversaries stampede vainly by while he stole the ball; then he would take all the time in the world to bring it out of the box. A man of imperturbable style, he was always whistling and looking the other way. He scorned speed. Master of suspense, lover of leisure, he would play in slow motion: the art of bringing the ball out slowly, calmly, was baptized *domingada*. When he finally let the ball go, he did so without ever running and without wanting to, because it saddened him to be left without her.

Domingos and She

This here ball helped me a lot. She or her sisters, right? It's a family to whom I owe a debt of gratitude. In my time on earth, she was the key. Because without her nobody plays at all. I started out in Bangu club's factory. Working, working, until I met my friend here. And I was very happy with her.

I've seen the world, traveled a lot, had many women. Women are a pleasure too, right?

(From an interview by Roberto Moura)

Goal by Atilio

It was 1939. Nacional from Montevideo and Boca Juniors from Buenos Aires were tied at two goals apiece and time was running out. Nacional was on the attack; Boca, in retreat, was holding them off. Then Atilio García got the ball, faced the jungle of legs, and opened up a path on the right, gobbling up the field, adversary by adversary.

Atilio was used to getting kicked. They would go after him with everything they had; his legs were a map of scars. That afternoon on the way to the goal, he was tackled hard by Angeletti and Suárez and had the pleasure of eluding them both twice. Valussi tore his shirt, grabbed him by the arm, and kicked him, and hefty Ibáñez blocked his path when he was running full tilt. But Atilio was unstoppable. The ball was part of his body and his body was a tornado, knocking over players as if they were rag dolls, until at last Atilio let the ball go with a terrifying smash that nearly burst the net.

The air smelled of gunpowder. Boca players surrounded the referee, demanding he disallow the goal because of the fouls *they* had committed. He paid them no heed, and the players left the field, indignant.

The Perfect Kiss Would Like to Be Unique

Quite a few Argentines swear, hand over heart, that Enrique García was the one. Known as "Bandyleg," García played left wing for the club Racing. Just as many Uruguayans swear, fingers crossed on their lips, that it was Pedro Lago, "Muleteer," a striker for Peñarol. It was one or the other, or perhaps both.

Half a century ago, or a little more, Lago or García scored a perfect goal, one that left his adversaries paralyzed with rage and admiration. Then he plucked the ball from the back of the net and with it under his arm he retraced his path, step by step, dragging his feet. That's right, raising lots of dust to erase his footsteps, so that no one could copy the play.

⊛ ⊛ ⊛ ⊛ ⊛ ⊛ ⊛ ⊛ ⊛ ⊛ ⊛ ⊛ ⊛ ⊛

The Machine

In the early 1940s, the Argentine club River Plate had one of the best soccer teams of all time.

"Some go in, others come out, everyone moves up, everyone falls back," explained Carlos Peucelle, one of the parents of this brood. The players traded places in a permanent rotation, defenders attacked, attackers defended: "On the blackboard and on the field," Peucelle liked to say, "our tactical plan is not the traditional 1–2–3–5. It's 1–10."

Even though everyone did everything on that River team, the forward line was the best. Muñoz, Moreno, Pedernera, Labruna, and Loustau played only eighteen matches together, but they made history and they still make for conversation. These five played by ear, whistling to each other to make their way upfield and to call to the ball, which followed like a happy dog and never lost its way.

People called that legendary team "The Machine" because of its precision plays. Dubious praise: these strikers had so much fun playing they'd forget to shoot at the goal. They had nothing in common with the mechanical coldness of a machine. Fans were fairer when they called them the "Knights of Anguish," because those bastards made their devotees sweat bullets before allowing them the relief of a goal.

Moreno

They called him "El Charro" because he looked like a Mexican movie star, but he was from the countryside upriver of Buenos Aires.

José Manuel Moreno, the most popular player on River's "Machine," loved to confound his opponents. His pirate legs would strike out one way but go another, his bandit head would promise a shot at one goalpost and drive it at the other.

Whenever an opponent flattened him with a kick, Moreno would get up by himself and without complaint, and no matter how badly he was hurt he would keep on playing. He was proud, a swaggerer and a scrapper who could punch out the entire enemy stands and his own as well, since his fans, though they adored him, had the nasty habit of insulting him every time River lost.

Lover of good music and good friends, man of the Buenos Aires night, Moreno used to meet the dawn tangled in someone's tresses or propped up on his elbows on the counter of some café.

"The tango," he liked to say, "is the best way to train: you maintain a rhythm, then change it when you stride forward, you learn the patterns, you work on your waist and your legs."

On Sundays at midday before each match, he would devour a big bowl of chicken stew and drain several bottles of red wine. Those in charge at River ordered him to give up his rowdy ways, unbecoming of a professional athlete. He did his best. For an entire week he slept at night and drank nothing but milk. Then he played the worst match of his life. When he went back to carousing, the club suspended him. His teammates went on strike in solidarity with this incorrigible Bohemian, and River had to play nine matches with replacements.

Let's hear it for partying: Moreno had one of the longest careers in the history of soccer. He played for twenty years in first–division clubs in Argentina, Mexico, Chile, Uruguay, and Colombia. When he returned from Mexico in 1946, River's fans were so anxious to see his daring thrusts and feints that they overflowed the stadium. His devotees knocked down the fences and invaded the playing field. He scored three goals and they carried him off on their shoulders. In 1952 Nacional in Montevideo made him a juicy offer, but he chose instead to play for another Uruguayan side, Defensor, a small club that could pay him little or nothing, because he had friends there. That year, Moreno stopped Defensor's decline.

In 1961 after retiring, he became coach of Medellín in Colombia. Medellín was losing a match against Boca Juniors from Argentina, and the players could not make any headway toward the goal. So Moreno, who was then forty-five, got out of his street clothes, took the field, and scored two goals. Medellín won.

Pedernera

"The penalty kick I blocked is going down in the history of Leticia," a young Argentine wrote in a letter from Colombia. His name was Ernesto Guevara and he was not yet "Che." In 1952 he was bumming around Latin America. On the banks of the Amazon, in Leticia, he coached a soccer team. Guevara called his traveling buddy "Pedernerita." He had no better way of praising him.

Adolfo Pedernera had been the fulcrum of River's "Machine." This one-man orchestra played every position, from one end of the forward line to the other. From the back he would create plays, thread the ball through the eye of a needle, change the pace, launch surprise breakaways; up front he would blow goalkeepers away.

The urge to play tickled him all over. He never wanted matches to end. When night fell, stadium employees would try in vain to get him to stop practicing. They wanted to pull him away from soccer but they couldn't: the game refused to him let go.

Goal by Severino

It was 1943. Boca Juniors was playing against River Plate's "Machine" in Argentina's soccer classic.

Boca was down by a goal when the referee whistled a foul at the edge of the River area. Sosa took the free kick. Rather than shoot on goal, he served up a center pass looking for Severino Varela's head. The ball came down way ahead of Varela. River's rear guard had an easy play; Severino was nowhere near it. But the veteran striker took off and flew through the air, clawing past several defenders until he connected with a devastating beret–blow that vanquished the goalkeeper.

His fans called him the "phantom beret" because he would fly uninvited into the goalmouth. Severino had years of experience and plenty of recognition with the Uruguayan club Peñarol by the time he went to Buenos Aires wearing the undefeated look of a mischievous child and a white beret perched on his skull.

With Boca he sparkled. Still, every Sunday at nightfall after the match, Severino would take the boat back to Montevideo, to his neighborhood, his friends, and his job at the factory.

Bombs

While war tormented the world, Rio de Janeiro's dailies announced a London blitz on the playing field of the club Bangu. In the middle of 1943, a match was to be played against São Cristovão, and Bangu's fans planned to send four thousand fireworks aloft, the largest bombardment in the history of soccer.

When the Bangu players took the field and the gunpowder thunder and lightning began, São Cristovão's manager locked his players in the dressing room and stuck cotton in their ears. As long as the fireworks lasted, and they lasted a long time, the dressing room floor shook, the walls shook, and the players shook too, all of them huddled with their heads in their hands, teeth clenched, eyes screwed shut, convinced that the World War had come home. Those who weren't epileptic must have had malaria, the way they were shaking when they stepped onto the field. The sky was black with smoke. Bangu creamed them.

A short while later, there was to be a match between the Rio de Janeiro and São Paulo teams. Once again, war clouds threatened and the dailies predicted another Pearl Harbor, a siege of Leningrad, and other cataclysms. The Paulistas knew that the loudest bang ever heard awaited them in Rio. Then the São Paulo manager had a brainwave: instead of hiding in the dressing room, his players would take the field at the same time as the Cariocas. That way instead of scaring them, the bombardment would be a greeting.

And that is what happened, only São Paulo lost anyway, 6–1.

The Man Who Turned Iron into Wind

Eduardo Chillida played goal for Real Sociedad in the Basque city of San Sebastián. Tall and skinny, he had a style of blocking shots that was his very own, and both Barcelona and Real Madrid had their eyes on him. The experts were predicting the boy would succeed Zamora.

But destiny had other plans. In 1943 a rival striker, appropriately named Sañudo, which means enraged, smashed Chillida's meniscus and everything else. After five operations on his knee, Chillida bid good-bye to soccer and became a sculptor.

Thus was born one of the greatest artists of the century. Chillida works with materials so heavy they sink into the earth, but his powerful hands toss iron and reinforced concrete into the air where they discover other spaces and create new dimensions on the fly. He used to do the same thing in the goal with his body.

Contact Therapy

Enrique Pichon-Rivière spent his entire life piercing the mysteries of human sadness and helping to crack open our cages of silence.

In soccer he found an effective ally. Back in the 1940s, Pichon-Rivière organized a team among his patients at the insane asylum. These locos were unbeatable on the playing fields of the Argentine littoral, and playing was their best therapy.

"Team strategy is my priority," said the psychiatrist, who was also the team's manager and top scorer.

Half a century later, we urban beings are all more or less crazy, even though due to space limitations nearly all of us live outside the asylum. Evicted by cars, cornered by violence, condemned to isolation, we live packed in ever closer to one another and feel ever more alone, with ever fewer meeting places and ever less time to meet.

In soccer, as in everything else, consumers are far more numerous than creators. Asphalt covers the empty lots where people used to pick up a match, and work devours our leisure time. Most people don't play, they just watch others play on television or from stands that lie ever farther from the field. Like Carnival, soccer has become a mass spectator sport. But just like Carnival spectators who start dancing in the streets, in soccer there are always a few admiring fans who kick the ball every so often out of sheer joy. And not only children. For better or for worse, though the fields are as far away as can be, friends from the neighborhood or work-mates from the factory, the office, or the faculty still get together to play for fun until they collapse exhausted. And then winners and losers go off together to drink and smoke and share a good meal, pleasures denied to the professional athlete.

Sometimes women take part too and score their own goals, though in general the macho tradition keeps them exiled from these fiestas of communication.

Goal by Martino

It was 1946. The Uruguayan club Nacional was beating San Lorenzo from Argentina, so they closed up their defensive lines to meet the threat from René Pontoni and Rinaldo Martino, players who were known for making the ball speak and who had the unfortunate habit of scoring.

Martino got to the edge of Nacional's area. There he retained the ball and caressed it as if he had all the time in the world. Suddenly Pontoni crossed like lightning toward the right corner. Martino paused, raised his head, looked at him. Then the Nacional defenders all jumped on Pontoni, and while the greyhounds pursued the rabbit Martino entered the box like a parrot into his cage, eluded the remaining fullback, shot, and scored.

The goal was Martino's but it also belonged to Pontoni, who knew how to confound the enemy.

Goal by Heleno

It was 1947. Botafogo against Flamengo in Rio de Janeiro. Botafogo striker Heleno de Freitas scored a chest goal.

Heleno had his back to the net. The ball flew down from above. He trapped it with his chest and whipped around without letting it fall. With his back arched and the ball still resting on his chest, he surveyed the scene. Between him and the goal stood a multitude. There were more people in Flamengo's area than in all Brazil. If the ball hit the ground he was lost. So Heleno started walking and calmly crossed the enemy lines with his body curved back and the ball on his chest. No one could knock it off him now without committing a foul, and he was in the goal area. When Heleno reached the goalmouth, he straightened up. The ball slid to his feet and he scored.

Heleno de Freitas was clearly a Gypsy. He had Rudolph Valentino's face and the temper of a mad dog. On the playing field, he sparkled.

One night at the casino he lost all his money. Another night, who knows where, he lost all his desire to live. And on his last night, delirious in a hospice, he died.

The 1950 World Cup

Color television was being born, computers were doing a thousand operations a second, and Marilyn Monroe was making her Hollywood debut. A movie by Buñuel, *Los Olvidados*, was capturing Cannes. Fangio's Formula One was winning in Monaco. Bertrand Russell was winning the Nobel. Neruda was publishing his *Canto General*, while Onetti and Octavio Paz were bringing out the first editions of *A Brief Life* and *The Labyrinth of Solitude*.

Pedro Albizu Campos, who had fought long and hard for Puerto Rico's independence, was being sentenced to seventy-nine years in prison in the United States. An informer had squealed on Salvatore Giuliano, the legendary bandit of southern Italy, and he lay dying, riddled by police bullets. In China, Mao's government was taking its first steps by outlawing polygamy and the sale of children. Wrapped in the flag of the United Nations, US troops were invading the Korean Peninsula with guns blazing, while soccer players were landing in Rio de Janeiro to vie for the fourth Rimet Cup after the long hiatus of the World War.

Taking part in the Brazilian tournament in 1950 were seven countries from the Americas and six from a Europe recently risen from the ashes. FIFA would not let Germany play. For the first time, England joined in the World Cup. Until then, the English had considered such skirmishes to be beneath them. The British side was defeated by the United States, believe it or not, and the goal that put the Americans over the top was the work not of

George Washington but of an immigrant from Haiti, a black center forward named Larry Gaetjens.

Brazil and Uruguay waged the final in Maracanã, the home team's new stadium, the largest in the world. Brazil was a sure winner; the final was going to be a party. Before the match began, the Brazilian players, who had crushed all comers with goal after goal, were given gold watches with "For the World Champions" engraved on the back. The front pages of the papers had been printed up in advance, the immense carnival float that would lead the victory parade was all set to go, half a million T-shirts with slogans celebrating the inevitable victory had already been sold.

When the Brazilian Friaça scored the first goal, the thunder of two hundred thousand voices and at least as many firecrackers shook the monumental stadium. But then Schiaffino rammed in the equalizer and a shot from the wing by Ghiggia gave Uruguay the championship with a 2–1 victory. When Ghiggia scored, the silence in Maracanã was deafening, the most raucous silence in the history of soccer, and Ary Barroso, the musician and composer of "Acuarela do Brasil," who was providing commentary on the match for the entire country, swore off broadcasting for good.

After the final whistle, Brazilian commentators called the defeat "the worst tragedy in Brazil's history." Jules Rimet wandered about the field like a lost soul, hugging the cup that bore his name: "I found myself alone with the cup in my arms and not knowing what to do. I finally found Uruguay's captain, Obdulio Varela, and I gave it to him practically without letting anyone else see. I held out my hand without saying a word."

In his pocket, Rimet had a speech he had written to congratulate the victorious Brazilians.

Uruguay had won cleanly: they committed eleven fouls to the Brazilians' twenty-one.

Third place went to Sweden, fourth to Spain. Brazil's Ademir led the list of scorers with nine goals, followed by the Uruguayan Schiaffino and the Spaniard Zarra with five apiece.

Obdulio

I was a little kid and a soccer fan, and like every other Uruguayan I was glued to the radio in 1950, listening to the World Cup final. When the voice of Carlos Solé broadcast the awful news of Brazil's first goal, my heart sank to the floor. Then I turned to my most powerful friend. I promised God a heap of sacrifices if He would appear in Maracaná and turn the match around.

I never managed to remember my many promises, so I couldn't keep them. Besides, although Uruguay's victory before the largest crowd ever assembled for a soccer match was certainly a miracle, it was the work of a flesh-and-blood mortal named Obdulio Varela. Obdulio cooled the match down when the steamroller came at us, and then he carried the entire team on his shoulders. By sheer courage he fought against all the odds.

At the end of the day, reporters surrounded the hero. Obdulio didn't stick out his chest or boast about being the best. "It was one of those things," he murmured, shaking his head. And when they wanted to take his picture, he turned his back.

He spent that night drinking beer in one Rio bar after another, his arm around the defeated fans. The Brazilians cried. No one recognized him. The next day he dodged the crowd that had turned out to meet him at the Montevideo airport, where an enormous billboard had his name in lights. In the midst of all the euphoria, he slipped away, dressed like Humphrey Bogart in a raincoat with the lapels turned up and a fedora pulled down to his nose.

The top brass of Uruguayan soccer rewarded themselves with gold medals. They gave the players silver medals and some cash. Obdulio's prize money was enough to buy a 1931 Ford. It was stolen a week later.

Barbosa

When it was time to select the best goalkeeper of the 1950 World Cup, journalists voted unanimously for the Brazilian Moacyr Barbosa. Without a doubt, Barbosa was the best keeper in the country, a man with springs in his legs whose calm self-assurance filled the entire team with confidence. He continued to be the best until he retired years later when he was in his forties. Over such a long career, who knows how many goals Barbosa blocked, and he never hurt a single striker.

But in that final match in 1950, the Uruguayan attacker Ghiggia surprised him with a bull's-eye from the right wing. Barbosa, who had come forward, leaped back and his fingers grazed the ball as he fell. He got up convinced that he had knocked the shot away and found the ball in the back of the net. That was the goal that left Maracanã Stadium dumbstruck and crowned Uruguay as champions.

Years went by and Barbosa was never forgiven. In 1993, during the qualifiers for the World Cup in the United States, he wanted to wish the Brazilian players well. He went to visit them at their training camp and those in charge would not let him in. By then he was dependent on the generosity of his sister-in-law, living in her home with nothing but a miserable pension. Barbosa commented: "In Brazil, the most you can get for any crime is thirty years. For forty-three years I've been paying for a crime I did not commit."

Goal by Zarra

It was at the World Cup in 1950. Spain was all over England, which only managed to shoot from afar.

Gaínza, on the wing, gobbled up the left side of the field, left half the defense sprawled on the ground, and lobbed a cross toward the English goal. Ramsey the fullback was turned around, his back to the ball, off balance, yet he managed to reach it. Then Zarra stampeded in and rammed it home off the left post.

Telmo Zarra, leading scorer in six Spanish championships, had inherited the adulation formerly bestowed on Manolete, the bullfighter. He played on three legs, the third being his devastating head. His best-known goals were headers. In 1950 Zarra did not score that winning goal with his head, but he certainly used it to celebrate loudly, while squeezing the little medal of the Immaculate Virgin that hung on his chest.

Top Spanish soccer official Armando Muñoz Calero, who had taken part in the Nazi invasion of Russia, sent a radio message to Generalissimo Franco: "Excellency: we have vanquished the perfidious Albion." Thus Spain finally got even for the defeat of the Invincible Armada in the waters of the English Channel in 1588.

Muñoz Calero dedicated the match "to the greatest Caudillo in the world." He didn't dedicate the next one to anyone. Spain faced Brazil and had to eat six goals.

Goal by Zizinho

Again, it was at the World Cup in 1950. In the match against Yugoslavia, Brazil's midfielder Zizinho scored a double goal.

This lord of soccer grace scored a clean goal and the referee disallowed it unfairly. So Zizinho repeated it step by step. He entered the box at the same spot, dribbled around the same Yugoslav defender with the same delicacy, slipping by on the left as before, and he drove the ball in at exactly the same angle. Then he kicked the ball angrily several times against the net.

The referee understood that Zizinho was capable of repeating that goal ten more times, and he had no choice but to allow it.

The Fun Lovers

Julio Pérez, one of the Uruguayan champions from 1950, used to cheer me up when I was a child. They called him "Pataloca," which means "Crazy Leg," because he could take himself apart in the air and leave his adversaries rubbing their eyes. They couldn't believe that his legs could fly one way while the rest of his body headed off in precisely the opposite direction. After eluding several opponents with such bodily taunts, he would back up and repeat the maneuver. In the stands we loved to cheer this party animal of the playing field, whose antics unleashed our laughter along with anything else that happened to be tied down.

Several years later I had the good luck to see the Brazilian Garrincha play, and he too had fun cracking jokes with his legs. Sometimes, when he was at the point of climax, he would back up, just to prolong the pleasure.

The 1954 World Cup

Gelsomina and Zampanò sprouted from Fellini's magic wand and were unhurriedly clowning around in *La Strada*, while Fangio was surging ahead to become Formula One world champion for the second time. Jonas Salk was concocting a vaccine against polio. In the Pacific the first hydrogen bomb was going off. In Vietnam General Giap was knocking out the French army in the decisive battle of Dien Bien Phu. In Algeria, another French colony, the war of independence was just beginning.

General Stroessner was being elected president of Paraguay in a close contest against himself. In Brazil the noose tied by businessmen and officers, money and guns, was tightening around President Getúlio Vargas and soon he would burst his heart with a bullet. US planes were bombing Guatemala with the blessing of the OAS, and an army created by that northern power was invading, killing, and winning. While in Switzerland the national anthems of sixteen countries were being sung to inaugurate the fifth World Cup, in Guatemala the victors were singing "The Star Spangled Banner" and celebrating the fall of President Arbenz, whose Marxist-Leninist ideology had been laid bare when he touched the lands of the United Fruit Company.

Taking part in the '54 World Cup were eleven teams from Europe and three from the Americas, plus Turkey and South Korea. Brazil unveiled its yellow shirt with a green collar to replace the white uniform that had brought them bad luck at Maracanã. But that canary color was no help at first: Brazil fell to Hungary in a violent match and did not even make the semifinals. The Brazilian delegation complained to FIFA about the British referee, who had acted "at the service of international communism against Western Christian civilization."

Hungary was the easy favorite to win this Cup. The steamroller combination of Puskás, Kocsis, and Hidegkuti had gone four years undefeated, and shortly before the World Cup they had crushed England 7–1. But it was no cakewalk. After the tough encounter with Brazil, the Hungarians threw everything they had at Uruguay. The two teams played to the death, neither giving any quarter, each wearing the other down, until at last two goals by Kocsis decided the match in extra time.

The final pitted Hungary against West Germany, whom the Hungarians had already walloped 8–3 at the beginning of the tournament when the captain, Puskás, was sidelined with an injury. In the final Puskás reappeared, barely scraping by on one leg, to lead a brilliant but exhausted team. Hungary was ahead 2–0 but ended up losing 3–2, and Germany won its first world title. Austria came in third, Uruguay fourth.

Kocsis the Hungarian was the leading scorer with eleven goals, followed by the German Morlock, the Austrian Probst, and the Swiss Hügi with six apiece. Of Kocsis's eleven goals, the most incredible was against Brazil. Kocsis took off like an airplane, went flying through the air, and headed the ball into the corner of the goal.

Goal by Rahn

It was at the World Cup in 1954. Hungary, the favorite, was playing West Germany in the final.

With six minutes left in a match tied 2–2, the robust German forward Helmut Rahn trapped a rebound from the Hungarian defense in the semicircle. Rahn evaded Lantos and fired a blast with his left, just inside the right post of the goal defended by Grosics.

Heribert Zimmermann, Germany's most popular broadcaster, announced that goal with a passion worthy of a South American: "*Tooooooooooorrrrrrrrrr!!!*"

It was the first World Cup Germany had been allowed to play since the war, and the German people again felt they had a right to exist. Zimmermann's cry became a symbol of national resurrection. Years later, that historic goal could be heard on the soundtrack of Fassbinder's film, *The Marriage of Maria Braun*, which recounts the misadventures of a woman who cannot find her way out of the ruins.

Walking Advertisements

In the mid-1950s, Peñarol signed the first contract for shirt ads. Ten players took the field with a company name displayed on their chests. Obdulio Varela, however, stuck with his old shirt. He explained: "They used to drag us blacks around by rings in our noses. Those days are gone."

Today, every soccer player is an advertisement in motion.

In 1989 Carlos Menem played a friendly match wearing the shirt of the Argentine national team, along with Maradona and the rest. On television it was hard to tell if he was the president of Argentina or Renault, whose enormous logo was featured on his chest.

In the '94 World Cup the Adidas and Umbro logos were more visible on players' shirts than any national symbol. The Mercedes-Benz star shines alongside the federal eagle on Germany's training uniform. That same star lights up the clothing of the club VfB Stuttgart. Bayern Munich, by contrast, prefers Opel cars. The packaging firm Tetra Pak sponsors Eintracht Frankfurt. Borussia Dortmund's players promote Continentale insurance, and Borussia Mönchengladbach's flog Diebels beer. The teams named for Bayer in Leverkusen and Uerdingen advertise the company's drugs Talcid and Larylin on their shirts.

The advertising on a player's chest is more important than the number on his back. In 1993 the Argentine club Racing, having no sponsor, published a desperate ad in the daily *Clarín*: "Wanted: *Sponsor* . . . " Advertising also outweighs the clean living the sport is supposed to promote. That same year, 1993, while fights in the stands in Chile reached such alarming proportions that the sale of alcohol during matches was banned, most of Chile's first-division teams were promoting beer or pisco on their shirts.

Speaking of clean living, a few years have gone by since the pope performed a miracle and turned the Holy Spirit into a bank. Now the Italian club Lazio has it for a sponsor: "Banco di Santo Spirito," proclaim their shirts, as if each player were one of God's tellers.

At the end of the second quarter of 1992, the Italian company Motta took stock of its accounts. Its logo, worn proudly on the chests of Club Milan's players, had been seen 2,250 times in newspaper photos and featured for six hours on television. Motta paid Milan $4.5 million, but its sales of cakes and other treats increased by $15 million over that period. Another Italian firm, Parmalat, which sells dairy products in forty countries, had a golden year in 1993. Its team, Parma, won the European Cup Winners' Cup for the first time, and in South America three teams that sport its logo on their shirts, Palmeiras, Boca, and Peñarol, won championships. Clambering over eighteen competitors, Parmalat took the Brazilian market by storm and gained a foothold among consumers in Argentina and Uruguay—all with a helping hand from soccer. What's more, along the way Parmalat bought several South American teams, thus acquiring not only shirts but legs. For $10 million, the company bought Edílson, Mazinho, Edmundo, Kléber, and Zinho, all of whom played or once played for the Brazilian national team, as well as the other seven players at the club Palmeiras. Anyone interested in acquiring them should write to the company's head office in Parma, Italy.

Ever since television started showing players up close, the entire uniform, from head to toe, has turned into a billboard. When a star takes his time tying his shoes, it's not slow fingers but pocketbook smarts: he is showing off the Adidas, Nike, or Reebok logo. Even back in the '36 Olympics organized by Hitler, the winning athletes featured Adidas's three stripes on their shoes. In the 1990 World Cup final between Germany and Argentina, Adidas's stripes were everywhere, including the ball and every strip of clothing worn by the players, the referee, and the linesmen. Two English journalists, Simson and Jennings, reported that only the referee's whistle didn't belong to Adidas.

Goal by Di Stéfano

It was 1957. Spain was playing Belgium.

Miguel caught the Belgian defense sleeping, penetrated on the right, and volleyed a crosskick to center. Di Stéfano leaped forward, diving full-length, and scored with a backheel from the air.

Alfredo Di Stéfano, the Argentine star who became a Spaniard, had a habit of scoring goals like that. Any open net was an unforgivable crime meriting immediate punishment, and he carried out the sentence by stabbing at it like a mischievous elf.

Di Stéfano

The entire playing field fit inside his shoes. From his feet it sprouted and grew. Alfredo Di Stéfano ran and reran the field from net to net. When he had the ball he would switch flanks and alter the pace, from a lazy trot to an unstoppable cyclone; when he didn't, he would evade his marker to gain open space, seeking air to keep a play from getting choked off.

He never stood still. Holding his head high, he could see the entire playing field and cross it at a gallop to pry open the defense and launch the attack. He was there at the beginning, the during, and the end of every scoring play, and he scored goals of all colors:

Watch out, watch out,
here comes the arrow
faster than all get out.

The crowd would carry him off the field on their shoulders.

Di Stéfano was the engine behind three teams that amazed the world in the 1940s: River Plate, where he took Pedernera's place; Millonarios from Bogotá, where he sparkled alongside Pedernera; and Real Madrid, where he was Spain's leading scorer five years in a row. In 1991, years after he retired, the magazine *France Football* bestowed on this Buenos Aires boy the title of "best European player of all time."

Goal by Garrincha

It was in Italy in 1958. Brazil's national team was playing Club Fiorentina on the way to the World Cup in Sweden.

Garrincha invaded the penalty area, left one defender sitting on his bottom, shook off another, and then one more. He eluded the goalkeeper too, then discovered another defender on the goal line. Garrincha made like he was going to shoot, then like he wasn't; he faked a kick at the near corner and the poor fellow crashed face first into the post. By then the goalkeeper was back. Garrincha put the ball between the keeper's legs and flew into the net along with it.

Afterward, with the ball under his arm, he slowly returned to the field. He walked with his gaze lowered, Chaplin in slow motion, as if asking forgiveness for the goal that had all Florence on its feet.

The 1958 World Cup

The United States was launching a satellite into the high heavens, a new little moon to circle the earth. It crossed paths with Soviet sputniks but never said hello. And while the great powers were competing in the Great Beyond, in the Here and Now civil war was breaking out in Lebanon, Algeria was burning, France was catching fire, and General de Gaulle was standing six feet tall above the flames and promising salvation. In Cuba Fidel Castro's general strike against the Batista dictatorship was failing, but in Venezuela another general strike was dooming the dictatorship of Pérez Jiménez. In Colombia, Conservatives and Liberals were at the polls to bless their deal to divvy up power after a decade of mutual extermination, while Richard Nixon was being welcomed with stones on his Latin American tour. *Deep Rivers* by José María Arguedas was being published, as were Carlos Fuentes's *Where the Air Is Clear* and Idea Vilariño's *Poemas de amor.*

In Hungary, Imre Nagy was being shot along with other rebels from '56 who wanted democracy instead of bureaucracy, and dying too were the Haitian rebels who had launched an assault on the palace where Papa Doc Duvalier reigned amid sorcerers and executioners. John XXIII, John the Good, was the new pope in Rome; Prince Charles was the future monarch of England; Barbie was the new queen of dolls. In Brazil João Havelange was conquering the throne in the industry of soccer, while in the art of soccer a seventeen-year-old kid named Pelé was being hailed king of the world.

The consecration of Pelé took place in Sweden during the sixth World Cup. Participating were twelve teams from Europe, four from the Americas, and none from other latitudes. Swedes could watch at the stadium or in their homes. This was the first Cup to be televised, although it was broadcast live only in Sweden. The rest of the world saw it later.

This was also the first time that a country playing outside its own continent won. At the beginning of the 1958 World Cup the Brazilians were nothing special, but after the players rebelled and convinced the coach to field the team they wanted, they were unstoppable. At that point five substitutes became starters, among them an unknown teenager named Pelé and Garrincha, who was already famous in Brazil and had sparkled in the qualifying matches but had been left off the starting line because psychological testing showed him to have a weak mind. These black second-stringers to white starters blazed with their own light in the new star team, along with another astonishing black, Didi, who organized their magic from the back.

Games and flames: the London paper *World Sports* said you had to rub your eyes to believe that it was of this world. In the semifinal against the French team of Kopa and Fontaine, the Brazilians won 5–2, and they won again 5–2 in the final against the home team. The Swedish captain, Liedholm, one of the cleanest and most elegant players in the history of soccer, converted the first goal of the match, but then Vavá, Pelé, and Zagallo put the

🏐 🏐 🏐 🏐 🏐 🏐 🏐 🏐 🏐 🏐 🏐 🏐 🏐 🏐

Swedes in their place under the astonished gaze of King Gustavus Adolphus. Brazil became champion without suffering a single defeat. When it was over, the victorious players gave the ball to their most devoted fan, the black masseur Américo.

France took third place and West Germany fourth. Fontaine of France led the list of scorers with a shower of thirteen goals, eight with the right leg, four with the left, and one with his head, followed by Pelé and Helmut Rahn of Germany who scored six apiece.

Goal by Nílton

I t was at the World Cup in 1958. Brazil was leading Austria 1–0. At the beginning of the second half, the key to the Brazilian defense, Nílton Santos, who was called "The Encyclopedia" for his vast knowledge of soccer, abandoned the rear guard, passed the center line, eluded a pair of opposing players, and kept going. The Brazilian manager, Vicente Feola, was also running but on the other side of the touchline. Sweating buckets he screamed, "Go back! Go back!"

Nílton, unflappable, continued his race toward the enemy area. A fat and desperate Feola clutched his head but Nílton refused to pass the ball to any of the forwards. He made the play entirely on his own and it culminated in a tremendous goal.

Then a happy Feola said, "Did you see that? Didn't I tell you? This one really knows!"

Garrincha

One of his many brothers baptized him Garrincha, the name of an ugly, useless little bird. When he started playing soccer, doctors made the sign of the cross. They predicted this misshapen survivor of hunger and polio, dumb and lame, with the brain of an infant, a spinal column like an S and both legs bowed to the same side, would never be an athlete.

There never was another right winger like him. In the 1958 World Cup he was the best in his position, in '62 the best player in the championship. But throughout his many years on the field, Garrincha was more: in the entire history of soccer no one made more people happy.

When he was playing, the field became a circus ring, the ball a tame beast, the game an invitation to a party. Like a child defending his pet, Garrincha would not let go of the ball, and together the ball and he would perform devilish tricks that had people in stitches. He would jump on her, she would hop on him, she would hide, he would escape, she would chase after him. In the process, the opposing players would crash into each other, their legs twisting around until they would fall, seasick, on their behinds. Garrincha did his rascal's mischief at the edge of the field, along the right touchline, far from the center; raised in the shantytown suburbs, that's where he preferred to play. His club was Botafogo, which means "firelighter," and he was the *botafogo* who fired up the fans crazed by firewater and all things fiery. He was the one who would climb out of the training camp window because he heard from some far-off back alley the call of a ball asking to be played with, music demanding to be danced to, a woman wanting to be kissed.

A winner? A loser with incredible luck. And luck doesn't last. As they say in Brazil, if shit was worth anything, the poor would be born without asses.

Garrincha died a predictable death: poor, drunk, and alone.

Didi

The press named him the best playmaker of the 1958 World Cup.

He was the hub of the Brazilian team. Lean body, long neck, poised statue of himself, Didi looked like an African icon standing at the center of the field, where he ruled. From there he would shoot his poison arrows.

He was a master of the deep pass, a near goal that would become a real goal on the feet of Pelé, Garrincha, or Vavá, but he also scored on his own. Shooting from afar, he used to fool goalkeepers with the "dry leaf": by giving the ball his foot's profile, she would leave the ground spinning and continue spinning on the fly, dancing about and changing direction like a dry leaf carried by the wind, until she flew between the posts precisely where the goalkeeper least expected.

Didi played unhurriedly. Pointing at the ball, he would say: "She's the one who runs."

He knew she was alive.

Didi and She

I always felt a lot of affection for her. Because if you don't treat her with affection, she won't obey. When she'd come, I'd take charge and she'd obey. Sometimes she'd go one way and I'd say, "Come here, child," and I'd bring her along. I'd take care of her blisters and warts and she'd always sit there, obedient as can be. I'd treat her with as much affection as I give my own wife. I had tremendous affection for her. Because she's fire. If you treat her badly, she'll break your leg. That's why I say, "Boys, come on, have some respect. This is a girl that has to be treated with a lot of love . . ." Depending on the spot where you touch her, she'll choose your fate.

(From an interview by Roberto Moura)

Kopa

They called him "the Napoleon of soccer" because he was short and he liked to conquer territory.

With the ball on his foot he grew taller and dominated the field. Raymond Kopa was a player of great mobility and florid moves, who would draw arabesques on the grass as he danced his way toward the goal. Coaches pulled their hair out watching him have so much fun with the ball, and French commentators often accused him of the crime of having a South American style. But at the '58 World Cup, the press named Kopa to the "dream team" and that year he won the Ballon d'Or for being the best player in Europe.

Soccer had pulled him out of misery. He started out on a team of miners. The son of Polish immigrants, Kopa spent his childhood at his father's side in the Noeux coal pits. He would go down every night and emerge the following afternoon.

Carrizo

He spent a quarter of a century catching balls with magnetic hands and sowing panic in the enemy camp. Amadeo Carrizo founded a style of South American play. He was the first goalkeeper who had the audacity to leave the penalty area and lead the attack. Heightening the danger, on more than one occasion this Argentine even took the enormous risk of dribbling past opposing players. Before Carrizo, such insanity was unthinkable. Then his audacity caught on. His compatriot Gatti, the Colombian Higuita, and the Paraguayan Chilavert also refused to resign themselves to the notion that the keeper is a living wall, glued to the net. They proved he can also be a living spear.

As we all know, fans delight in hating the enemy: rival players always deserve condemnation or scorn. But Argentine fans of all stripes praise Carrizo, and all but one or two agree that on that country's playing fields no one ever blocked shots as well as he did. Nevertheless, in 1958 when the Argentine team returned with their tails between their legs after the World Cup in Sweden, it was the idol who caught the most heat. Argentina had been beaten by Czechoslovakia 6–1, and such a misdeed demanded a public expiation. The press pilloried him, the crowds hissed and whistled, and Carrizo was crushed. Years later in his memoirs he confessed sadly: "I always recall the goals they scored on me rather than the shots I blocked."

❧ ❧ ❧ ❧ ❧ ❧ ❧ ❧ ❧ ❧ ❧ ❧ ❧ ❧

Shirt Fever

Uruguayan writer Paco Espínola did not like soccer. But one afternoon in the summer of 1960, when he was scanning the radio dial for something to listen to, he chanced upon the local classic. Peñarol was routed by Nacional 4–0.

When night fell, Paco felt so depressed he decided to eat alone so as not to embitter the life of anyone else. Where did all that sadness come from? Paco was prepared to believe there was no particular reason, maybe the sheer sorrow of being mortal. Suddenly it hit him: he was sad because Peñarol had lost. He was a Peñarol fan and hadn't known it.

How many Uruguayans were sad like him? And how many, on the other hand, were jumping with joy? Paco experienced a delayed revelation. Normally we Uruguayans *belong* to Nacional or to Peñarol from the day we are born. People say, for example, "I'm with Nacional." That's the way it has been since the beginning of the twentieth century. They say that back then the professionals of love used to attract clients by sitting in the doorways of Montevideo's bordellos wearing nothing but the shirts of Peñarol or Nacional.

For the fanatic, pleasure comes not from your own club's victory, but from the other's defeat. In 1993 a Montevideo daily interviewed a group of young men who supported themselves by carrying firewood all week and enjoyed themselves by screaming for Nacional in the stadium on Sundays. One of them confessed, "For me, just the sight of a Peñarol shirt makes me sick. I want them to lose every time, even when they play against foreigners."

It's the same story in other divided cities. In 1988 in the final of the Copa América, Nacional beat Newell's, one of two clubs that share the adoration of the city of Rosario on the Argentine littoral. On that occasion the fans of the other club, Rosario Central, filled the streets of their city to celebrate the defeat of Newell's at the hands of a foreign team.

I think it was Osvaldo Soriano who told me the story of the death of a Boca Juniors fan in Buenos Aires. That fan had spent his entire life hating the club River Plate, as was entirely appropriate, but on his deathbed he asked to be wrapped in the enemy flag. That way he could celebrate with his final breath the death of "one of them."

If the fan *belongs* to a club, why not the players? Rarely will a fan accept an idol in a new venue. Changing clubs is not the same as changing workplaces, although the player is indeed a professional who earns his living by his legs. Loyalty to the uniform does not fit with modern soccer, but the fans still mete out punishment for the crime of desertion. In 1989, when the Brazilian player Bebeto left Flamengo for Vasco da Gama, some Flamengo fans went to Vasco da Gama matches just to boo the traitor. Threats rained down on him and the most fearful sorcerer in Rio de Janeiro put a hex on him. Bebeto suffered a rosary of injuries; he could not play without getting hurt or without guilt weighing down his legs. Things went from bad to worse until he gave up and left for Spain. Some years earlier the longtime star of the Argentine club Racing, Roberto Perfumo, moved over to River Plate. His loyal fans gave him one of the longest and loudest catcalls in history. "I realized how much they loved me," Perfumo said.

Nostalgic for the faithful old days, fans also are loath to accept the calculations of profitability that often determine managers' decisions, now that every club has been obliged to become a factory for producing extravaganzas. When business is not going well, red ink cries out for sacrificing some of the company's assets. A gigantic Carrefour supermarket now sits on the ruins of San Lorenzo's stadium in Buenos Aires. When the stadium was demolished in the middle of 1983, weeping fans carried off fistfuls of dirt in their pockets.

The club is the only identity card fans believe in. And in many cases the shirt, the anthem, and the flag embody deeply felt traditions that may find expression on the playing field but spring from the depths of a community's history. For Catalonians, the Barcelona team is more than a club; it is a symbol of their long struggle for national affirmation against the central power in Madrid. Since 1919 no foreigners and no non-Basque Spaniards have played for Athlétic in Bilbao. A bastion of Basque pride, Athlétic only takes Basque players into its ranks, and they are nearly always players from their own farm teams. During the long dictatorship of Franco, two stadiums, Camp Nou in Barcelona and San Mamés in Bilbao, were sanctuaries for outlawed nationalist sentiment. There, Catalonians and Basques could shout and sing in their own languages and wave their outlawed flags. The first time the Basque standard was raised without provoking a beating from the police was in a soccer stadium. A year after Franco's death, the players of Athlétic and Real Sociedad carried the flag onto the field.

Yugoslavia's war of disintegration, which so upset the entire world, began on the soccer field before it took to the battlefield. The ancient resentment between Serbs and Croats came to the surface every time clubs from Belgrade and Zagreb faced each other. Fans revealed their deep passions and dug up flags and chants from the past to use as battle-axes.

Goal by Puskás

It was 1961. Real Madrid was playing at home against Atlético of Madrid.

No sooner had the match begun than Ferenc Puskás scored a double goal, just as Zizinho had in the 1950 World Cup. The Hungarian striker for Real Madrid executed a free kick at the edge of the box and the ball went in. But as Puskás celebrated with his arms in the air, the referee went up to him. "I'm sorry," he apologized, "but I didn't whistle."

So Puskás shot again. He kicked with his left foot, as before, and the ball traveled exactly the same path: like a cannonball over the same heads of the same players in the wall and, just like the goal that had been disallowed, it landed in the upper left corner of the net tended by Madinabeytia, who leaped just as before and, as before, was unable even to graze it.

Goal by Sanfilippo

*D*ear Eduardo,

I've got to tell you about this. The other day I went to the Carrefour supermarket, the one built where San Lorenzo used to play. I was with my childhood hero José Sanfilippo, who was San Lorenzo's leading scorer four seasons in a row. There we were, walking among the shopping carts, surrounded by pots and pans and cheese and strings of sausage. All of a sudden, as we head for the checkout, Sanfilippo opens his arms and says: "To think that it was right here where I rammed it in on Roma with a half-volley in that match against Boca." He walks in front of a housewife pushing a cart filled to the brim with cans, steaks, and vegetables, and he says: "It was the fastest goal in history."

He concentrates, as if he were waiting for a corner kick, and he says to me: "I told the center-half, a young fellow, 'As soon as the ball is in play send it to me in the box. Don't worry, I won't make you look bad.' I was older and this kid, Capdevilla was his name, was scared, thinking, 'What if I don't come through?'" And then Sanfilippo points to a stack of mayonnaise jars and screams: "He put it right here!" People are looking at us like we're nuts. "The ball came down behind the halfbacks, I stumbled but it landed ahead of me there where the rice is, see?" He points to the bottom shelf, and all of a sudden he starts running like a rabbit in spite of his blue suit and shiny shoes. "I let it bounce and boom!" He swings his left leg in a tremendous kick. We all spin around to look at the checkout, where the goal sat thirty-odd years ago, and it's as if we all see the ball hit the net up high, right by the batteries and the razor blades. Sanfilippo raises his arms to celebrate. The shoppers and the checkout girls pound their hands applauding. I'm practically in tears. "Baby" Sanfilippo scored that goal from 1962 all over again, just so I could see it.

Osvaldo Soriano

The 1962 World Cup

A few Indian and Malaysian astrologists were predicting the end of the world, but it kept on turning, and as it turned an organization with the name of Amnesty International was born and Algeria took its first steps of independent life after more than seven years of war against France. In Israel the Nazi criminal Adolf Eichmann was being hanged, the miners of Asturias were on strike, and Pope John was trying to change the Church and return it to the poor. They were making the first computer disks and performing the first operations with laser beams, and Marilyn Monroe was losing her will to live.

What was the price of a country's vote? Haiti sold its franchise for $15 million, a highway, a dam, and a hospital, and that's how the OAS got a majority to expel Cuba, the black sheep of Pan-Americanism. Well-informed sources in Miami were announcing the imminent fall of Fidel Castro, it was only a matter of hours. Seventy-five suits were being launched in US courts to ban the novel *Tropic of Cancer* by Henry Miller, published for the first time in an unexpurgated edition. Linus Pauling, who was about to win his second Nobel Prize, was picketing the White House to protest nuclear testing, while Benny "The Kid" Paret, an illiterate black Cuban, was dying, beaten to a pulp, in the ring at Madison Square Garden.

In Memphis Elvis Presley was announcing his retirement after selling 300 million records, but before long he changed his mind, while in London a record company, Decca, was refusing to record the songs of a group of hairy musicians who called themselves The Beatles. Carpentier was publishing *Explosion in the Cathedral*, Gelman was publishing *Gotán*, the Argentine military were overthrowing President Frondizi, and the Brazilian painter Cândido Portinari was dying. *Primeiras estórias* by Guimarães Rosa was in the bookstores, as were the poems that Vinícius de Moraes wrote *para viver um grande amor*. João Gilberto was crooning "One Note Samba" in Carnegie Hall, while the Brazilian soccer team was landing in Chile, expecting to win the seventh World Cup against five other countries from the Americas and ten from Europe.

Luck was not with Di Stéfano in the '62 World Cup. He was going to play for his adopted country, Spain. At thirty-six this would be his last opportunity. Just before the opening match, he hurt his right knee and there was no way he could play. Di Stéfano, "The Blond Arrow," one of the best players in the history of soccer, never played in a World Cup. Pelé, another all-time star, did not get far in Chile either: he pulled a muscle early on and could not play. And one more sacred giant of soccer, the Russian Yashin, also turned into a lame duck. The best goalkeeper in the world let in four goals by Colombia, because, it seems, he bucked himself up with a few too many nips in the dressing room.

Brazil won the tournament without Pelé and under Didi's charge. Amarildo sparkled in the difficult role of filling Pelé's shoes, Djalma Santos made himself into a wall on defense, and up front Garrincha was inspired and inspiring. "What planet is Garrincha from?" asked the daily *El Mercurio*, when Brazil liquidated the home team. The Chileans had beaten Italy in a match that was a pitched battle, and they also beat Switzerland and the Soviet Union. They gobbled up the spaghetti, chocolate, and vodka, but choked on the coffee: Brazil won 4–2.

In the final, Brazil downed Czechoslovakia 3–1 and, just as in '58, was the undefeated champion. For the very first time the World Cup final was broadcast live internationally on television, although in black and white and only to a few countries.

Chile won third place, its best ranking ever, and Yugoslavia won fourth thanks to a bird named Dragoslav Sekularac whom no defender could catch.

The championship did not have a leading scorer, but several players notched up four goals: Garrincha and Vavá of Brazil, Sánchez of Chile, Jerkovic of Yugoslavia, Albert of Hungary, and Ivanov of the Soviet Union.

Goal by Charlton

It happened at the World Cup in 1962. England was playing against Argentina.

Bobby Charlton set up the first English goal by placing the ball where Flowers could face the goalkeeper Roma alone. But the second goal was Charlton's from start to finish. Charlton, lord of the entire left side of the field, made the Argentine defense collapse like swatted moths. He changed feet at full tilt and using his right he overwhelmed the keeper with a shot from the wing.

Bobby was a survivor. Practically all the players on his team, Manchester United, died in the twisted ruins of a burning plane. Death spared this miner's son so he could continue giving people the high nobility of his soccer.

The ball obeyed him. She traveled the field following his instructions and flew into the net before he even kicked her.

Yashin

When Lev Yashin covered the goal, not a pinhole was left open. This giant with long spidery arms always dressed in black and he played with a naked elegance that disdained the spectacle of unnecessary gestures. He liked to stop thundering blasts with a single claw-like hand that trapped and shredded all projectiles, while his body remained motionless like a rock. He could deflect the ball with a glance.

He retired from soccer several times, always pursued by torrents of gratitude, and several times he returned. There was no other like him. During more than a quarter of a century, this Russian blocked more than a hundred penalty shots and saved who-knows-how-many goals. When asked for his secret, he would say the trick was to have a smoke to calm your nerves, then toss back a strong drink to tone your muscles.

Goal by Gento

It was 1963. Real Madrid faced Pontevedra.

As soon as the referee blew the opening whistle, there was a goal by Di Stéfano. Then right at the beginning of the second half Puskás scored. From that point on, the fans waited in suspense for the next goal, which would be number 2,000 for Real Madrid since it started playing in the Spanish League in 1928. Madrid fans invoked the goal by kissing their fingers while making the sign of the cross, and the enemy fans warded it off by pointing their index and little fingers at the ground.

The game turned around. Pontevedra began to dominate. When night fell and only a few minutes remained, and that goal so desired and so feared seemed lost from sight, Amancio fired off a dangerous free kick: Di Stéfano couldn't reach the ball but it was trapped by Gento. The Madrid left winger broke free of the defenders surrounding him, shot and won. The stadium went wild.

All rival teams were on the lookout to capture Francisco Gento, the fugitive. Sometimes they managed to put him behind bars, but he always escaped.

Seeler

A jolly face. You could not imagine him without a mug of foaming beer in his fist. On Germany's soccer fields he was always the shortest and the stoutest: a pudgy pink hamburger with an unsteady gait, because one foot was larger than the other. But Uwe Seeler was a flea when he jumped, a hare when he ran, and a bull when he headed the ball.

In 1964 this center forward for Hamburg was chosen as the best player in Germany. He belonged to Hamburg body and soul: "I'm just another fan. Hamburg is my home," he liked to say. Uwe Seeler scorned numerous juicy offers to play on Europe's most powerful teams. He played in four World Cups. To shout "Uwe, Uwe" was the best way of shouting "Germany, Germany."

Matthews

In 1965, when he was fifty years old, Stanley Matthews still caused serious outbreaks of hysteria in British soccer. There weren't enough psychiatrists to deal with all the victims, who had been perfectly normal until the cursed moment they were bewitched by this grandfatherly tormentor of fullbacks.

Defenders would grab his shirt or his shorts, they would get him in wrestling holds or tackle him with kicks worthy of the police blotter, nothing stopped him because they never managed to clip his wings. Matthews was precisely that, a winger, the one who flew highest over England's turf, all along the touchlines.

Queen Elizabeth was well aware of this: she made him a knight.

The 1966 World Cup

The military was bathing Indonesia in blood, half a million, a million, who-knows-how-many dead, and General Suharto was inaugurating his long dictatorship by murdering the few reds, pinks, or questionables still alive. Other officers were overthrowing Nkrumah, president of Ghana and prophet of African unity, while their colleagues in Argentina were evicting President Illia by coup d'état.

For the first time in history a woman, Indira Gandhi, was governing India. Students were toppling Ecuador's military dictatorship. The US Air Force was bombing Hanoi with renewed vigor, but Americans were growing ever more convinced they should never have gone into Vietnam, let alone stayed, and should leave as soon as possible.

Truman Capote had just published *In Cold Blood*. García Márquez's *One Hundred Years of Solitude* and Lezama Lima's *Paradiso* were in the bookstores. The priest Camilo Torres was dying in battle in the mountains of Colombia, Che Guevara was riding his skinny Rocinante through Bolivia's countryside, and Mao was unleashing the Cultural Revolution in China. Several atomic bombs were falling on the Spanish coast at Almería, sowing panic even though none of them went off. Well-informed sources in Miami were announcing the imminent fall of Fidel Castro, it was only a matter of hours.

In London, with Harold Wilson chewing his pipestem and celebrating victory at the polls, young women sporting miniskirts, Carnaby Street as fashion capital, and the entire world humming Beatles tunes, the eighth World Cup got under way.

This was the final World Cup for Garrincha and it was also a good-bye party for Mexican goalkeeper Antonio Carbajal, the only player to be in the tournament five times.

Sixteen teams took part: ten from Europe, five from the Americas, and, strange as it seems, North Korea. Astonishingly, the Koreans eliminated Italy with a goal by Pak, a dentist from the city of Pyongyang who played soccer in his spare time. On the Italian squad were no less than Gianni Rivera and Sandro Mazzola. Pier Paolo Pasolini used to say they played soccer in lucid prose interspersed with sparkling verse, but that dentist left them speechless.

For the first time the entire championship was broadcast live by satellite and, though in black and white, the whole world could watch the show put on by the referees. In the previous World Cup, European referees officiated at twenty-six matches; in this one, they ran twenty-four out of thirty-two. A German referee gave England the match against Argentina, while an English referee gave Germany the match against Uruguay. Brazil had no better luck: Pelé was hunted down and kicked with impunity by Bulgaria and Portugal, which knocked Brazil out of the championship.

Queen Elizabeth attended the final. She did not scream when players scored, but she did applaud discreetly. The World Cup came down to the England of Bobby Charlton, a man of fearful drive and marksmanship, and the Germany of Beckenbauer, who had just begun his career and was already playing with hat, gloves, and cane. Someone had stolen the Rimet Cup, but a dog named Pickles found it in a London garden, and the trophy reached the winner's hands in time. England won 4–2. Portugal came in third, the Soviet Union fourth. Queen Elizabeth gave Alf Ramsey, the manager of the victorious team, a title of nobility, and Pickles became a national hero.

The '66 World Cup was usurped by defensive tactics. Every team used the sweeper system with an extra defender by the goal line behind the fullbacks. Even so, Eusebio, Portugal's African artilleryman, managed to pierce those impenetrable rearguard walls nine times. Behind him on the list of leading scorers was Haller of Germany with six.

Greaves

In a western he would have been the fastest foot in the West. On the soccer field he scored a hundred goals before he was twenty, and by the time he was twenty-five they still hadn't invented a lightning rod that could ground him. More than run, he exploded: Jimmy Greaves pushed off so fast the referees used to call him offside by mistake, because they could not figure out where his sudden stabs and bull's-eye shots came from. They would see him land, but they never saw him take off.

"I want to score so badly," he said, "it hurts."

Greaves had no luck at the '66 World Cup. He did not score a single goal, and an attack of jaundice made him sit out the final.

Goal by Beckenbauer

It happened at the World Cup in 1966. Germany was playing Switzerland.

Uwe Seeler launched the attack along with Franz Beckenbauer, the two of them like Sancho Panza and Don Quixote, the ball fired by an invisible trigger, back and forth, yours and mine. Once the entire Swiss defense was left useless as a deaf ear, Beckenbauer faced the goalkeeper Elsener, who leaped to his left. Beckenbauer pivoted at full tilt, shot to the opposite side, and in it went.

Beckenbauer was twenty and that was his first goal in a World Cup. After that he took part in four more, as player or manager, and never finished below third place. Twice he raised the Rimet Cup: playing in '74 and managing in '90. Bucking the trend toward a soccer of sheer panzer-style strength, he proved that elegance can be more powerful than a tank and delicacy more penetrating than a howitzer.

This emperor of the midfield, known as "The Kaiser," was born in a working-class section of Munich, but he commanded both attack and defense with nobility. In the back nothing escaped him: not one ball, not a fly, not a mosquito could get through. And when he crossed the field he was like fire.

Eusebio

He was born to shine shoes, sell peanuts, or pick pockets. As a child they called him "Ninguém": no one, nobody. Son of a widowed mother, he played soccer from dawn to dusk with his many brothers in the empty lots of the shantytowns.

He set foot on the field running as only someone fleeing the police or poverty nipping at his heels can run. That's how he became champion of Europe at the age of twenty, sprinting in zigzags. They called him "The Panther."

At the World Cup in 1966, his long strides left adversaries scattered on the ground, and his goals, from impossible angles, set off cheers that never ended.

Portugal's best player ever was an African from Mozambique. Eusebio: long legs, dangling arms, sad eyes.

꩜ ꩜ ꩜ ꩜ ꩜ ꩜ ꩜ ꩜ ꩜ ꩜ ꩜ ꩜ ꩜ ꩜

The Curse of the Posts

The keeper had a face chiseled with an ax and pitted by smallpox. His huge gnarled hands bolted and padlocked the net, and his feet shot off cannonballs. Of all the Brazilian goalkeepers I've ever seen, Manga is the one I remember most. Once, in Montevideo, I saw him score a goal from net to net: Manga kicked from his goal and the ball went into the opponents' goal without any other player touching it. He was playing for the Uruguayan club Nacional as a penance after having been driven out of Brazil. The Brazilian team went home shamefaced from the '66 World Cup, where they suffered an ignominious defeat, and Manga was the scapegoat of that national disgrace. He had played in only one match. He made a mistake, got drawn out and, as bad luck would have it, Portugal scored on the empty net. That unfortunate error became such a scandal that for a long time mistakes by goalkeepers were known as *mangueiradas*.

Something like that happened at the '58 World Cup, when the keeper Amadeo Carrizo paid the price for Argentina's defeat. And before that, in 1950, when Moacyr Barbosa was the whipping boy for Brazil's loss in the final at Maracanã.

At the 1990 World Cup Cameroon unseated Colombia, which had just won a brilliant match against Germany. The African team's winning goal came on a foolish mistake by the goalkeeper René Higuita, who took the ball up to midfield and lost it there. The same people who like to cheer such audacity when it turns out well wanted to eat Higuita alive when he got back home.

In 1993 the Colombian team, without Higuita, crushed Argentina 5–0 in Buenos Aires. Such a humiliation cried out for someone to blame, and the guilty party had to be—who else?—the goalkeeper. Sergio Goycoechea paid for all the broken dishes. The Argentine team had been undefeated in more than thirty matches, and in each one Goycoechea was the key to its success. But after Colombia's goalfest the miracle penalty-blocker not only lost his nickname, Saint Goyco, he also lost his spot on the team. More than one fan recommended suicide.

Peñarol's Glory Years

In 1966 the champions of the Americas and Europe, Peñarol and Real Madrid, faced each other twice. With fancy dribbling, beautiful plays, and barely any sweat on their shirts, Peñarol won both matches 2–0.

In the 1960s, Peñarol inherited the scepter from Real Madrid, the greatest team of the previous decade. Peñarol won the Inter-Continental Cup twice in those years and was champion of the Americas three times.

When the best squad in the world took the field, they warned the opposing players: "Did you bring another ball? This one belongs to us."

The ball was forbidden entry to Mazurkiewicz's net, in the midfield she obeyed the orders of "Tito" Gonçalves, and up front she buzzed on the feet of Spencer and Joya. At "Pepe" Sasía's command, she would pierce the goal. But she had fun too, especially when Pedro Rocha would swing her back and forth.

Goal by Rocha

It was 1969. Peñarol was playing Estudiantes from La Plata. Rocha was at the center of the field, marked by two players, with his back to the enemy area, when he got the ball from Matosas. He put it to sleep on his right foot, spun around with the ball still there, slipped it behind his other foot, and escaped his markers Echecopar and Taverna. He made three quick dashes, left the ball to Spencer, and continued running. The return pass came in high in the semicircle. He trapped it with his chest, broke free of Madero and Spadaro, and volleyed a shot before it hit the ground. The goalkeeper, Flores, did not even see it.

Pedro Rocha slithered along like a snake in the grass. He played joyfully and his joy was infectious: the joy of the play, the joy of the goal. He did whatever he wanted with the ball, and she believed every bit of it.

My Poor Beloved Mother

At the end of the 1960s, poet Jorge Enrique Adoum returned to Ecuador after a long absence. As soon as he arrived, he performed an obligatory ritual in the city of Quito: he went to the stadium to see the Aucas play. It was an important match and the stands were packed.

Before the kickoff there was a minute of silence for the referee's mother, who had died that morning. Everyone stood, everyone was silent. Then someone made a speech praising the dedication of this exemplary sportsman who was going to officiate, performing his duty even in the most difficult of circumstances. At the center of the field, his head bowed, the man in black acknowledged the sustained applause of the crowd. Adoum blinked, he pinched himself: he couldn't believe it. What country was he in? So much had changed. Before, people's only concern for the referee was to call him a son of a bitch.

And the match began. At fifteen minutes Aucas scored and the stadium exploded. But the referee disallowed the goal due to an offside, and the thoughts of the crowd turned immediately to his deceased mater: "Orphan of a bitch!" roared the stands.

Tears Do Not Flow from a Handkerchief

Soccer, metaphor for war, at times turns into real war. Then "sudden death" is no longer just a name for a dramatic way of deciding a tied match. These days, soccer fanaticism has come to occupy the place formerly reserved for religious fervor, patriotic ardor, and political passion. As often occurs with religion, patriotism, and politics, soccer can bring tensions to a boil, and many horrors are committed in its name.

Some believe men possessed by the demon of the ball foam at the mouth, and frankly that image presents a fairly accurate picture of the frenzied fan. But even the most indignant of critics would concede that in most cases violence does not originate in soccer, any more than tears flow from a handkerchief.

In 1969 war broke out between Honduras and El Salvador, two small and very poor Central American countries that for more than a century had been accumulating reasons to distrust one another. Each had always served as the magical explanation for the other's problems. Hondurans have no work? Because Salvadorans come and take their jobs. Salvadorans are hungry? Because Hondurans mistreat them. Both countries believed their neighbor was the enemy, and the relentless military dictatorships of each did all they could to perpetuate the error.

This war was called the Soccer War because the sparks that set off the conflagration were struck in the stadiums of Tegucigalpa and San Salvador. The trouble began during the qualifying rounds for the 1970 World Cup. There were tussles, a few injuries, several deaths. A week later, the two countries broke off relations. Honduras expelled a hundred thousand Salvadoran peasants who had always worked in that country's plantings and harvests; Salvadoran tanks crossed the border.

The war lasted a week and killed four thousand people. The two governments, dictatorships forged at a US factory called the School of the Americas, fanned the fires of mutual hatred. In Tegucigalpa the slogan was "Honduran, don't sit still, grab a stick and a Salvadoran kill." In San Salvador: "Teach those barbarians a lesson." The lords of land and war did not lose a drop of blood, while two barefoot peoples avenged their identical misfortunes by killing each other with abandon.

Goal by Pelé

It was 1969. Santos was playing Vasco da Gama in Maracaná Stadium. Pelé crossed the field in a flash, evading his opponents without ever touching the ground, and when he was about to enter the goal along with the ball, he was tripped.

The referee whistled a penalty. Pelé did not want to take it. A hundred thousand people forced him to, screaming out his name.

Pelé had scored many goals in Maracaná. Prodigious goals, like the one in 1961 against Fluminense when he dribbled past seven defenders and the keeper as well. But this penalty was different; people felt there was something sacred about it. That's why the noisiest crowd in the world fell silent. The clamor disappeared as if obeying an order: no one spoke, no one breathed. All of a sudden the stands seemed empty and so did the playing field. Pelé and the goalkeeper, Andrada, were alone. By themselves, they waited. Pelé stood by the ball resting on the white penalty spot. Twelve paces beyond stood Andrada, hunched over at the ready, between the two posts.

The goalkeeper managed to graze the ball, but Pelé nailed it to the net. It was his thousandth goal. No other player in the history of professional soccer had ever scored a thousand goals.

Then the multitude came back to life and jumped like a child overjoyed, lighting up the night.

Pelé

A hundred songs name him. At seventeen he was champion of the world and king of soccer. Before he was twenty the government of Brazil named him a "national treasure" not to be exported. He won three world championships with the Brazilian team and two with the club Santos. After his thousandth goal, he kept on counting. He played more than thirteen hundred matches in eighty countries, one after another at a punishing rate, and he scored nearly thirteen hundred goals. Once he held up a war: Nigeria and Biafra declared a truce to see him play.

To see him play was worth a truce and a lot more. When Pelé ran hard, he cut right through his opponents like a hot knife through butter. When he stopped, his opponents got lost in the labyrinths his legs embroidered. When he jumped, he climbed into the air as if it were a staircase. When he executed a free kick, his opponents in the wall wanted to turn around to face the net, so as not to miss the goal.

He was born in a poor home in a far-off village, and he reached the summit of power and fortune where blacks were not allowed. Off the field he never gave a minute of his time and a coin never fell from his pocket. But those of us who were lucky enough to see him play received alms of extraordinary beauty: moments so worthy of immortality that they make us believe immortality exists.

The 1970 World Cup

In Prague cinema puppet master Jiří Trnka was dying; so was Bertrand Russell in London, after nearly a century of very lively living. After only twenty years, the poet Rugama was dying too, in Managua, fighting alone against a battalion from the Somoza dictatorship. The world was losing its music: the Beatles were breaking up thanks to an overdose of success, and thanks to an overdose of drugs guitarist Jimi Hendrix and singer Janis Joplin were also taking their leave.

A hurricane was ripping through Pakistan and an earthquake was wiping out fifteen cities in the Peruvian Andes. In Washington, though no one believed in the Vietnam War anymore, it kept dragging on, with the death toll reaching one million, according to the Pentagon, and the generals fleeing forward by invading Cambodia. After losing in three previous attempts, Allende was launching another campaign for the presidency of Chile, promising milk for every child and nationalization of the nation's copper.

Well-informed sources in Miami were announcing the imminent
fall of Fidel Castro, it was only a matter of hours. For the first
time in history, the Vatican was on strike. While employees of the
Holy Father in Rome were crossing their arms, in Mexico players
from sixteen countries were moving their legs and the ninth
World Cup got under way.

Nine teams from Europe, five from the Americas, plus Israel
and Morocco took part. In the first match, the referee raised a yellow card for the first time. The yellow card, sign of warning, and
the red card, sign of expulsion, were not the only novelties at the
Mexico World Cup. The rules now allowed for two substitutions
during the course of each match. Before, only the goalkeeper
could be replaced in case of injury, and it was never very hard to
reduce the adversary's numbers with a few well-placed kicks.

Images of the 1970 World Cup: the impression left by Beckenbauer as he battled to the final minute with one arm in a sling;
the fervor of Tostão, fresh from an eye operation and managing a
sure-footed performance in every match; the aerobatics of Pelé in
his final World Cup: "We jumped together," said Burgnich, the
Italian defender who marked him, "but when I landed, I could
see Pelé was still floating in the air."

Four world champions—Brazil, Italy, West Germany, and
Uruguay—faced off in the semifinals. Germany took third place,
Uruguay fourth. In the final, Brazil astonished Italy 4–1. The
British press commented, "Such beautiful soccer ought to be outlawed." People stand up to tell the story of the final goal: the ball
traveled through all Brazil, each of the eleven players touched it,
and at last Pelé, without even looking, laid it out on a silver platter for Carlos Alberto coming in like a tornado to make the kill.

"Torpedo" Müller from Germany led the list of scorers with
ten, followed by the Brazilian Jairzinho with seven.

Undefeated champions for the third time, Brazil kept the
Rimet Cup for good. At the end of 1983 the cup was stolen and
sold after being melted down to nearly two kilos of pure gold. In
the display case, a replica stands in its place.

Goal by Jairzinho

It was at the 1970 World Cup. Brazil was playing England.
Tostão got the ball from Paulo Cézar and scurried ahead as far
as he could, but all of England was spread out in the penalty
area. Even the Queen was there. Tostão eluded one, then another
and one more, then he passed the ball to Pelé. Three players suffocated him on the spot. Pelé pretended to press on and the three
opponents went for the smoke. He put on the brakes, pivoted,
and left the ball on the feet of Jairzinho, who was racing in. Jairzinho had learned to shake off his markers on sandlots in the
toughest slums of Rio de Janeiro. He came on like a black bullet
and evaded one Englishman before the ball, a white bullet,
crossed the goal line defended by the keeper Banks.

It was the winning goal. Swaying to the rhythm of a fiesta,
Brazil's attackers had tossed off seven guardians of the steel
fortress, which simply melted under the hot breeze blowing from
the south.

⚽ ⚽ ⚽ ⚽ · ⚽ ⚽ ⚽ ⚽ ⚽ ⚽ ⚽ ⚽ **155**

The Fiesta

There are towns and villages in Brazil that have no church, but not a one lacks a soccer field. Sunday is the day of hard labor for cardiologists all over the country. On a normal Sunday people die of excitement during the mass of the ball. On a Sunday without soccer, people die of boredom.

When the Brazilian national team met disaster at the '66 World Cup, there were suicides, nervous breakdowns, flags at half-staff, and black ribbons on doors. A procession of dancing mourners filled the streets to bury the country's soccer prowess in a coffin. Four years later, Brazil won the world championship for the third time and Nelson Rodrigues wrote that Brazilians were no longer afraid of being carried off by the dogcatcher, they were all ermine-caped kings in pointy crowns.

At the World Cup in 1970, Brazil played a soccer worthy of her people's yearning for celebration and craving for beauty. The whole world was suffering from the mediocrity of defensive soccer, which had the entire side hanging back to maintain the *catenaccio*, while one or two men played by themselves up front. Risk and creative spontaneity were not allowed. Brazil, however, was astonishing: a team on the attack, playing with four strikers—Jairzinho, Tostão, Pelé, and Rivelino—sometimes increased to five and even six when Gérson and Carlos Alberto came up from the back. That steamroller pulverized Italy in the final.

A quarter of a century later, such audacity would be considered suicide. At the '94 World Cup, Brazil won another final against Italy, this time decided in a penalty shootout after 120 minutes without a single goal. If it had not been for the penalty shots, the nets would have remained untouched for all eternity.

Soccer and the Generals

A t the victory carnival in 1970, General Médici, dictator of Brazil, handed out cash to the players, posed for photographers with the trophy in his arms, and even headed a ball for the cameras. The march composed for the team, "Forward Brazil," became the government's anthem, while the image of Pelé soaring above the field was used in TV ads proclaiming "No one can stop Brazil." When Argentina won the World Cup in 1978, General Videla used the image of Kempes, unstoppable as a hurricane, for exactly the same purpose.

Soccer is the fatherland, soccer is power: "I am the fatherland," these military dictators were saying.

Meanwhile, Chile's bigwig General Pinochet named himself president of Colo-Colo, the most popular club in the country, and General García Meza, who had taken over Bolivia, named himself president of Wilstermann, a club with a multitude of fervent fans.

Soccer is the people, soccer is power: "I am the people," these military dictators were saying.

Don't Blink

Eduardo Andrés Maglioni, forward for the Argentine club Independiente, won a spot in the *Guinness Book of World Records* as the player who scored the most goals in the least time.

In 1973, at the beginning of the second half of a match against Gimnasia y Esgrima from La Plata, Maglioni beat the goalkeeper Guruciaga three times in a minute and fifty seconds.

Goal by Maradona

It was 1973. The youth teams of Argentinos Juniors and River Plate were playing in Buenos Aires.

Number 10 for Argentinos received the ball from his goalkeeper, evaded River's center forward, and took off. Several players tried to block his path: he put it over the first one's head, between the legs of the second, and he fooled the third with a backheel. Then, without a pause, he paralyzed the defenders, left the keeper sprawled on the ground, and walked the ball to the net. On the field stood seven crushed boys and four more with their mouths agape.

That kid's team, the Cebollitas, went undefeated for a hundred matches and caught the attention of the press. One of the players, "Poison," who was thirteen, declared, "We play for fun. We'll never play for money. When there's money in it, everybody kills themselves to be a star and that's when jealousy and selfishness take over."

As he spoke he had his arm around the best-loved player of all, who was also the shortest and the happiest: Diego Armando Maradona, who was twelve and had just scored that incredible goal.

Maradona had the habit of sticking out his tongue when he was on the attack. All his goals were scored with his tongue out. By night he slept with his arms around a ball and by day he performed miracles with it. He lived in a poor home in a poor neighborhood and he wanted to be an industrial engineer.

The 1974 World Cup

President Nixon was hanging from the ropes, weak-kneed, buffeted ceaselessly by the Watergate scandal, while a spaceship was hurtling toward Jupiter and in Washington an army lieutenant who had murdered a hundred civilians in Vietnam was being found innocent. After all, there weren't more than a hundred, and they were civilians, and what's more, they were Vietnamese.

The novelists Miguel Ángel Asturias and Pär Lagerkvist lay dying, along with the painter David Alfaro Siqueiros. General Perón, who had burned his mark on Argentina's history, was on his deathbed. Dying too was Duke Ellington, the king of jazz. The daughter of the king of the press, Patricia Hearst, was falling in love with her kidnappers, robbing banks, and denouncing her father as a bourgeois pig. Well-informed sources in Miami were announcing the imminent fall of Fidel Castro, it was only a matter of hours.

The dictatorship in Greece was crumbling, and so was the one in Portugal, where the Carnation Revolution was dancing to the beat of "Grândola, vila morena." The dictatorship of Augusto Pinochet was tightening its grip on Chile, while in Spain Francisco Franco was dying in the Francisco Franco Hospital, sick with power and age.

In a historic plebiscite, Italians were voting to legalize divorce, which seemed preferable to daggers, poison, and other methods favored by tradition for resolving marital disputes. In a no less historic vote in Switzerland, the leaders of world soccer were electing João Havelange president of FIFA, ousting the prestigious Stanley Rous, while in Germany the tenth World Cup was getting under way.

A brand-new cup was on display. Though uglier than the Rimet Cup, it was nonetheless coveted by nine teams from Europe and five from the Americas, plus Australia and Zaire. The Soviet Union had lost out in the run-up for refusing to play a qualifying-round match in Chile's National Stadium, which not long before had been a concentration camp and the site of executions by firing squad. So, in that stadium the Chilean team played the most pathetic match in the history of soccer: it played against no one and scored several goals on the empty net to cheers from the crowd. In the World Cup, Chile did not win a single match.

Surprise: the Dutch players brought their wives or girlfriends with them to Germany and stayed with them throughout the tournament. It was the first time such a thing had happened. Another surprise: the Dutch had wings on their feet and reached the final undefeated, with fourteen goals in their favor and only one against, which out of sheer bad luck had been scored by one of their own. The 1974 World Cup revolved around the "Clockwork Orange," the overwhelming creation of Cruyff, Neeskens, Rensenbrink, Krol, and the other indefatigable Dutch players driven by coach Rinus Michels.

At the beginning of the final match, Cruyff exchanged pennants with Beckenbauer. And then the third surprise occurred: the Kaiser and his team punctured the Dutch party balloon. Maier who blocked everything, Müller who scored everything, and Breitner who solved everything poured two buckets of cold water on the favorites, and against all odds the Germans won 2–1. Thus the history of the '54 Cup in Switzerland, when Germany beat the unbeatable Hungary, was repeated.

Behind West Germany and the Netherlands came Poland. In fourth place Brazil, which did not manage to be what it could have been. One Polish player, Lato, ended up as leading scorer with seven, followed by another Pole, Szarmach, and the Dutchman Neeskens with five apiece.

Cruyff

They called the Dutch team the "Clockwork Orange," but there was nothing mechanical about this work of the imagination that had everyone befuddled with its incessant changes. Like River's "Machine," another team libeled by its nickname, this orange fire flitted back and forth, fanned by an all-knowing breeze that sped it forward and pulled it back. Everyone attacked and everyone defended, deploying and retreating in a vertiginous fan. Faced with a team in which each one was all eleven, the opposing players lost their step.

A Brazilian reporter called it "organized disorganization." The Netherlands had music, and the one who carried the melody, keeping so many simultaneous notes on pitch and in tune, was Johan Cruyff. Conducting the orchestra and playing his own instrument at the same time, Cruyff worked harder than anyone.

This scrawny livewire earned a spot on the Ajax roster when he was only a child: while his mother waited tables at the club bar, he collected balls that went off the field, shined the players' shoes, and placed the flags in the corners. He did everything they asked of him and nothing they ordered him to do. He wanted to play and they would not let him because his body was too weak and his will too strong. When they finally gave him a chance, he took it and never let it go. Still a boy, he made his debut, played stupendously, scored a goal, and knocked out the referee with one punch.

From that night on he kept up his reputation for being tempestuous, hardworking, and talented. Over two decades he won twenty-two championships in the Netherlands and Spain. He retired when he was thirty-seven; after scoring his final goal, the crowd carried him on its shoulders from the stadium to his house.

Müller

The coach of Club TSV in Munich told him, "You won't go far in soccer. Better try something else."

Back then, Gerd Müller worked twelve hours a day in a textile mill.

Eleven years later, in 1974, this stumpy tub of a player was champion of the world. No one scored more goals than he in the history of either the German league or the national team.

Disguised as an old woman, his fangs and claws hidden, the wild wolf on the field strolled along unseen, making a show of showering innocent passes and other works of charity. Meanwhile, he slipped unnoticed into the box. The net was the bridal veil of an irresistible girl. In front of the open goal he licked his chops. And in one fell swoop he stood naked, then bit.

꩜ ꩜ ꩜ ꩜ ꩜ ꩜ ꩜ ꩜ ꩜ ꩜ ꩜ ꩜ ꩜

Havelange

In 1974, after a long climb, Jean-Marie Faustin Goedefroid de Havelange reached FIFA's summit and announced: "I have come to sell a product named soccer."

From that point on, Havelange has exercised absolute power over the world of soccer. His body glued to the throne, Havelange reigns in his palace in Zurich surrounded by a court of voracious technocrats. He governs more countries than the United Nations, travels more than the pope, and has more medals than any war hero.

Havelange was born in Brazil, where he owns Cometa, the country's largest bus and trucking company, and other businesses specializing in financial speculation, weapons sales, and life insurance. But his opinions do not seem very Brazilian. A journalist from the *Times* of London once asked him: "What do you like best about soccer? The glory? The beauty? The poetry? Winning?"

And he answered: "The discipline."

This old-style monarch has transformed the geography of soccer and made it into one of the more splendid multinational businesses in the world. Under his rule, the number of countries competing in world championships has doubled: there were sixteen in 1974, and there will be thirty-two as of 1998. And from what we can decipher through the fog surrounding his balance sheets, the profits generated by these tournaments have multiplied so prodigiously that the biblical miracle of bread and fish seems like a joke in comparison.

The new protagonists of world soccer—countries in Africa, the Middle East, and Asia—offer Havelange a broad base of support, but his power gains sustenance, above all, from his association with several gigantic corporations, Coca-Cola and Adidas among them. It was Havelange who convinced Adidas to finance the candidacy of his friend Juan Antonio Samaranch for the presidency of the International Olympic Committee in 1980. Samaranch, who during the Franco dictatorship had the good sense to wear a blue shirt and salute with his palm extended, is now the other king of world sport. These two manage enormous sums of money. How much, no one knows. They are rather bashful about the subject.

The Owners of the Ball

FIFA, which holds court in Zurich, the International Olympic Committee, which rules from Lausanne, and the company ISL Marketing, whose orders issue from Lucerne, manage the World Cup and the Olympics. All three of these powerful organizations maintain their head offices in Switzerland, a country famous for William Tell's marksmanship, precision watches, and religious devotion to bank secrecy. Coincidentally, all three profess an extraordinary degree of modesty when it comes to the money that passes through their hands and the money that in their hands remains.

ISL Marketing owns exclusive rights over stadium advertising, films and videos, logos, banners, and mascots for international soccer competitions until the end of the century. This business belongs to the heirs of Adolf Dassler, founder of Adidas, brother and enemy of the founder of its competitor Puma. When Havelange and Samaranch offered a sales monopoly to the Dassler family, they were acting out of gratitude, a noble sentiment. Adidas, the largest sports clothing manufacturer in the world, had shown considerable generosity when it came to helping them consolidate their own personal power. In 1990 the Dasslers sold Adidas to French businessman Bernard Tapie, but held on to ISL, which the family runs in association with the Japanese advertising firm Dentsu.

Control over world sport is no small potatoes. At the end of 1994, speaking in New York to a business association, Havelange confessed a few numbers, something he rarely does: "I can confirm that soccer generates a total of $225 billion worldwide every year." He boasted that such a fortune compared favorably to the $136 billion in sales that General Motors, the world's largest multinational corporation, recorded in 1993.

In the same speech, Havelange warned, "Soccer is a commercial product that must be sold as wisely as possible." And he cited the first law of wisdom in today's world: "You have to pay a lot of attention to the packaging."

The sale of television rights is the most productive vein in the fantastically rich mine of international competitions, and FIFA and the International Olympic Committee enjoy the lion's share of the proceeds. That money has multiplied spectacularly since television began to broadcast world championships live around the world. The 1992 Barcelona Olympics earned 630 times as much from television as the Rome Olympics in 1960, when the broadcast did not reach beyond the national market.

When it comes to choosing the advertisers for each tournament, Havelange, Samaranch, and the Dassler family never quarrel. The machine that turns every passion into money cannot afford the luxury of promoting the most healthy or useful products for active sports fans. They simply place themselves at the service of the highest bidder, and they only want to know if MasterCard will pay more than Visa, and if Fujifilm will put more money on the table than Kodak. Coca-Cola, that nutritious elixir

no athlete's body can do without, always heads the list. Its wealth
of virtues places it beyond question.

With fin de siècle soccer so wrapped up in marketing and
sponsors, it's no surprise that some of Europe's biggest clubs are
actually companies that belong to other companies. Juventus
from Turin, just like Fiat, is part of the Agnelli Group. Milan belongs to the constellation of three hundred companies of the
Berlusconi Group. Parma belongs to Parmalat. Sampdoria, to the
oil conglomerate Mantovani. Fiorentina, to the movie production
company Cecchi Gori. Olympique de Marseilles moved to the
forefront of European soccer when it became one of Bernard
Tapie's companies, until a bribery scandal ruined his successful career. Paris Saint-Germain belongs to the television firm Canal
Plus. Sochaux's sponsor, Peugeot, also owns the club stadium.
Philips owns the Dutch club PSV in Eindhoven. Bayer is the
name of the two German first-division clubs the company fi-
nances: Bayer Leverkusen and Bayer Uerdingen. The inventor and
owner of Amstrad computers is also the proprietor of the British
club Tottenham Hotspur, whose shares are traded on the stock exchange. Blackburn Rovers belongs to Walkersteel magnate Jack
Walker.

In Japan, where professional soccer is still young, the largest
companies have set up their own teams and hired foreign stars,
making the safe bet that soccer is a universal language for advertising their businesses the world over. Furukawa electric company
started the club Jef United Ichihara and hired German superstar

Pierre Littbarski and the Czechs František and Pavel. Toyota set up Club Grampus and signed on English striker Gary Lineker. The veteran but ever-brilliant Zico played for Kashima, which belongs to the Sumitomo industrial-financial conglomerate. Mazda, Mitsubishi, Nissan, Panasonic, and Japan Airlines also have soccer teams.

The teams may lose money, but that does not matter as long as they project a good image for their corporate proprietors. That's why their ownership is no secret: soccer helps advertise the companies and in all the world there is no greater public relations tool. When Silvio Berlusconi bought Milan, which was in bankruptcy, he launched a new chapter in the club's life with all the choreography of a major advertising campaign. That afternoon in 1987, Milan's eleven players descended slowly from a helicopter hovering above the center of the field while loudspeakers blared Wagner's "Ride of the Valkyries." Bernard Tapie, another specialist in his own protagonism, liked to celebrate Olympique's victories with huge parties glowing with fireworks and laser beams, where top rock groups performed.

◈ ◈ ◈ ◈ ◈ ◈ ◈ ◈ ◈ ◈ ◈ ◈ ◈ ◈

Soccer, the fountain of so much passion, also generates fame and power. The teams that enjoy some autonomy, because they do not depend directly on other companies, are often run by shady businessmen or second-rate politicians who use the game as a prestigious platform to catapult themselves into the public eye. There are also rare cases where just the opposite is true: men who put their well-earned fame at the service of soccer, like the English singer Elton John who took over Watford, the team he loved, or the movie director Francisco Lombardi, who runs Peru's Sporting Cristal.

[As tends to happen in the cutthroat business of professional sports, a number of teams have changed hands and some of the companies have gone belly up since this book was first published in 1995. Parma, Sampdoria, Fiorentina, Paris Saint-Germain, Uerdingen, and Tottenham are all owned by different corporate behemoths. And ISL Marketing collapsed without warning in 2001, at which point the International Olympic Committee discovered it could sell TV rights very well on its own, thank-you. But the essence of the story remains unchanged: few hands own the ball that captivates the world.]

Jesus

In the middle of 1969, a large hall for weddings, baptisms, and conventions opened in Spain's Guadarrama Mountains. While the grand opening banquet was in full swing, the floor collapsed, the roof fell in, and the guests were buried in rubble. Fifty-two people died. The hall had been built with public funds but without proper authorization, a building permit, or an architect in charge.

The owner and builder of the ephemeral edifice, Jesus Gil y Gil, went to jail. He got two years, three months, and two weeks behind bars for each death, but was eventually pardoned by Generalissimo Franco. As soon as he stepped out of prison, Jesus was back to serve the progress of the fatherland once again in the construction industry.

Some time later, this businessman became the owner of a soccer team, Atlético of Madrid. Thanks to soccer, which turned him into a popular television personality, this Jesus was able to launch a political career. In 1991 he was elected mayor of Marbella, winning more votes than anyone else in the country. During his election campaign he promised to clear pickpockets, drunks, and drug addicts off the streets of this tourist town reserved for the amusement of Arab sheiks and foreign gangsters specializing in gunrunning and drug trafficking.

Atlético of Madrid remains the foundation of his power and prestige, even though the team loses all too frequently. Managers do not last more than a few weeks. Jesus Gil y Gil seeks advice from his horse Imperioso, a snow-white and very sentimental stallion: "Imperioso, we lost."

"I know, Gil."

"Whose fault is it?"

"I don't know, Gil."

"Yes you do, Imperioso. It's the manager's fault."

"So, fire him."

The 1978 World Cup

In Germany the popular Volkswagen Beetle was dying, in England the first test tube baby was being born, in Italy abortion was being legalized. The first victims of AIDS, a disease not yet called that, were succumbing. The Red Brigades were killing Aldo Moro, and the United States was promising to give Panama back the canal it had stolen at the beginning of the century. Well-informed sources in Miami were announcing the imminent fall of Fidel Castro, it was only a matter of hours. In Nicaragua the Somoza dynasty was teetering, as was the Shah's in Iran. The Guatemalan military was machine-gunning a crowd of peasants in the town of Panzós. Domitila Barrios and four other women from tin-mining communities were launching a hunger strike against Bolivia's military dictatorship, and soon all Bolivia would be on a hunger strike: the dictatorship was falling. The Argentine military dictatorship, in contrast, was enjoying good health and, to prove it, was playing host to the eleventh World Cup.

Ten European countries, four from the Americas, plus Iran and Tunisia took part. The pope sent his blessings from Rome. To the strains of a military march, General Videla pinned a medal on Havelange during the opening ceremonies in Buenos Aires's Monumental Stadium. A few steps away, Argentina's Auschwitz, the torture and extermination camp at the School of Navy Mechanics, was operating at full speed. A few miles beyond that, prisoners were being thrown alive from airplanes into the sea.

"At last the world can see the true face of Argentina," crowed the president of FIFA to the TV cameras. Special guest Henry Kissinger predicted, "This country has a great future in all ways." And the captain of the German team, Berti Vogts, who made the first kickoff, declared a few days later, "Argentina is a country where order reigns. I haven't seen a single political prisoner."

The home team won a few matches, but lost to Italy and drew with Brazil. To reach the final against the Netherlands, it had to drown Peru in a flood of goals. Argentina got more than it needed, but the massacre, 6–0, sowed doubt among skeptical fans and magnanimous ones alike. The Peruvians were stoned on their return to Lima.

The final between Argentina and the Netherlands was decided in extra time. The Argentines won 3–1 and in a way their victory was due to the patriotism of the post that saved the Argentine net in injury time. That post, which stopped a resounding blast by Rensenbrink, was never given military honors only because of the nature of human ingratitude. In any case, more important than the post, as it turned out, were the goals of Mario Kempes, an unbreakable bronco who liked to gallop over the grass carpeted in a snowfall of confetti, his shaggy mane flying in the wind.

When they handed out the trophies, the Dutch players refused to salute the leaders of the Argentine dictatorship. Third place went to Brazil, fourth to Italy.

Kempes was voted best player in the Cup and was also the leading scorer with six goals. Behind him came the Peruvian Cubillas and Rensenbrink of the Netherlands with five apiece.

Happiness

F ive thousand journalists from all over the world, a sumptu-
ous media center, impeccable stadiums, gleaming new airports: Argentina was a model of efficiency. Veteran German
reporters confessed that the '78 World Cup reminded them of the
'36 Olympics in Berlin, when Hitler pulled out all the stops.

The cost was a state secret. Many millions of dollars were
spent and lost—how many, it was never known—so that the
smiles of a happy country under military tutelage would be
broadcast to the four corners of the earth. Meanwhile, the top
brass who organized the World Cup carried on with their plan of
extermination, for reasons of war or just to be sure. "The final so-
lution," as they called it, murdered thousands of Argentineans
without leaving a trace—how many, it was never known. Anyone
who tried to find out was swallowed up by the earth. Curiosity,
like dissent, like any question, was absolute proof of subversion.
The president of the Argentine Rural Society, Celedonio Pereda,
declared that thanks to soccer, "there will be no more of the
defamation that certain well-known Argentineans have spread
through the Western media with the proceeds from their

robberies and kidnappings." You could not criticize the players, not even the manager. The Argentine team stumbled a few times in the championship, but local commentators were obliged to do nothing but applaud.

To make over its international image, the dictatorship paid an American public relations firm half a million dollars. The report from the experts at Burson-Marsteller was titled *What Is True for Products, Is Also True for Countries.* Admiral Carlos Alberto Lacoste, the strongman of the World Cup, explained in an interview: "If I go to Europe or to the United States, what will impress me most? Tall buildings, huge airports, terrific cars, fancy candies . . . "

The admiral, an illusionist skilled at making dollars evaporate and sudden fortunes appear, took the reins of the World Cup after the previous officer in charge was mysteriously assassinated. Lacoste managed immense sums of money without any oversight, and because he wasn't paying close attention, it seems he ended up keeping some of the change. Even the dictatorship's own finance minister, Juan Alemann, took note of the squandering of public funds and asked a few inconvenient questions. The admiral had the habit of warning: "Don't complain if later on somebody plants a bomb."

A bomb did explode in Alemann's house at the very moment when Argentineans were celebrating their fourth goal against Peru.

When the Cup was over, in gratitude for his hard work, Admiral Lacoste was named vice president of FIFA.

Goal by Gemmill

It happend at the World Cup in 1978. The Netherlands, which was doing well, was playing Scotland, which was doing poorly. Scottish player Archibald Gemmill got the ball from his countryman Hartford and kindly asked the Dutch to dance to the tune of a lone bagpiper.

Wildschut was the first to fall, his head spinning, at Gemmill's feet. Then Gemmill left Suurbier reeling in the dust. Krol had it worse: Gemmill put it between his legs. And when the keeper Jongbloed came at him, the Scot lobbed the ball over his head.

❀ ❀ ❀ ❀ ❀ ❀ ❀ ❀ ❀ ❀ ❀ ❀ ❀ ❀

Goal by Bettega

It also happened at the '78 World Cup. Italy defeated the home team 1–0.

The play that set up Italy's goal drew a perfect triangle on the playing field; inside, the Argentine defenders were left as lost as blind men in a shootout. Antognoni slid the ball over to Bettega, who slapped it toward Rossi, who had his back to him. Rossi returned it with a backheel while Bettega infiltrated the box. Bettega then overpowered two players and beat the keeper Fillol with a tremendous left.

Though no one knew it then, the Italian team had already begun to win the World Cup that would take place four years later.

Goal by Sunderland

It was 1979. At Wembley Stadium, Arsenal and Manchester United were battling the final of the English FA Cup.

A good match, but nothing aroused suspicions that this would turn on a dime into the most electric final in the Cup's long history since 1871. Arsenal was ahead 2–0 and time was running out. The match was essentially decided and people began to leave the stadium. A sudden cloudburst of goals, *three in two minutes*: a sure shot by McQueen was followed by a pretty penetration by McIlroy, who eluded two defenders and the keeper, giving Manchester the equalizers in the 86th and 87th minutes. And before the 88th minute was over, Arsenal had regained the lead. Liam Brady, who was as usual the outstanding player of the match, put together the final play, and Alan Sunderland took a clean shot to make it 3–2.

The 1982 World Cup

Mephisto by István Szabó, a masterpiece on art and betrayal, was winning an Oscar in Hollywood, while in Germany the life of the tormented and talented movie director Fassbinder was being snuffed out early. Romy Schneider was committing suicide and Sophia Loren was being imprisoned for tax evasion. In Poland, union leader Lech Walesa was on his way to jail.

García Márquez was accepting the Nobel Prize in the name of the poets, beggars, musicians, prophets, warriors, and rascals of Latin America. In a village in El Salvador, a hail of army bullets was killing more than seven hundred peasants, half of them children. In order to expand the butchery of Indians, in Guatemala General Ríos Montt was taking power by force, proclaiming that God had given him the country's reins and announcing that the Holy Spirit would direct his secret service.

Egypt was recovering the Sinai Peninsula, occupied by Israel since the Six Day War. The first artificial heart was beating in someone's breast. Well-informed sources in Miami were announcing the imminent fall of Fidel Castro, it was only a matter of hours. In Italy the pope was surviving a second assassination attempt. In Spain the officers who had organized the attack on Congress were getting thirty years and Felipe González was launching his unerring race for the presidency, while in Barcelona the twelfth World Cup was getting under way.

Twenty-four countries took part, eight more than in the previous Cup, but the Americas did not gain a larger quota: there were fourteen teams from Europe, six from the Americas, and two from Africa, plus Kuwait and New Zealand.

On the first day in Barcelona, world champion Argentina went down to defeat. A few hours later, very far from there, off in the Falkland Islands, the Argentine generals were routed in their war against England. These ferocious fighters, who over several years of dictatorship had won the war against their own countrymen, surrendered like lambs to the British. The image was broadcast on television: navy officer Alfredo Astiz, violator of every human right, hung his head and signed the humiliating surrender.

During the days that followed, TV showed images of the '82 Cup: the billowing tunic of Sheik Fahad Al-Ahmed Al-Jaber Al-Sabah, who ran onto the field to protest a goal by France against

Kuwait; the goal by Englishman Bryan Robson after half a minute, the quickest in World Cup history; the indifference of German keeper Schumacher, who once was a blacksmith, after he knocked out French striker Battiston with his knee.

Europe won the top spots in the tournament, although Brazil played the best soccer on the feet of Zico, Falcão, and Sócrates. Luck was not with the Brazilians, but they delighted the crowd and Zico, who had just won the title of best player in South America, justified once again the "Zicomania" in the stands.

The Cup went to Italy. The Italian team started off badly, stumbling from draw to draw, but finally took flight, thanks to its overall cohesion and the opportune machine-gun blasts of Paolo Rossi. In the final against Germany, Italy won 3–1.

Poland, guided by Boniek's fine music, took third place. Fourth went to France, which deserved better for the European effectiveness and African joy of its memorable midfield.

The Italian Rossi led the list of scorers with six goals, followed by the German Rummenigge, who scored five and set the team on fire.

Pears from an Elm

Alain Giresse, along with Platini, Tigana, and Genghini, made up the most spectacular midfield of the '82 World Cup and in the entire history of French soccer. Giresse was so small that on the TV screen he always appeared to be far away.

The Hungarian Puskás was short and fat like the German Seeler. The Dutchman Cruyff and the Italian Gianni Rivera were skinny. Pelé had flat feet, as did Néstor Rossi, Argentina's solid center half. The Brazilian Rivelino scored worst on the Cooper test, but on the field no one could catch him. His countryman Sócrates had the body of a heron, long bony legs and small feet that tired easily, but he was such a master of the backheel he even used it for penalty kicks.

Whoever believes physical size and tests of speed or strength have anything to do with a soccer player's prowess is sorely mistaken. Just as mistaken as those who believe that IQ tests have anything to do with talent or that there is a relationship between penis size and sexual pleasure. Good soccer players need not be titans sculpted by Michelangelo. In soccer, ability is much more important than shape, and in many cases skill is the art of turning limitations into virtues.

The Colombian Carlos Valderrama has warped feet, and the curvature helps him hide the ball. It's the same story with Garrincha's twisted feet. Where is the ball? In his ear? Inside his shoe?

Where did it go? The Uruguayan "Cococho" Alvarez, who walked with a limp, had one foot pointing toward the other, and he was one of the few defenders who could stop Pelé without punching or kicking him.

Two short chubby players, Romário and Maradona, were the stars of the '94 World Cup. And two Uruguayan strikers who later on became stars in Italy, Ruben Sosa and Carlos Aguilera, have a similar physique. Thanks to their diminutive size, the Brazilian Leônidas, the Englishman Kevin Keegan, the Irishman George Best, and the Dane Allan Simonsen, known as "The Flea," all managed to slip through impenetrable defenses and scurry easily by huge fullbacks who hit them with all they had but could not stop them. Also tiny but well armored was Félix Loustau, left winger for River Plate's "Machine." They called him "The Ventilator" because he was the one who allowed the rest of the squad to catch their breath by making the opposing players chase him. Lilliputians can change speed and accelerate brusquely without falling because they aren't built like skyscrapers.

Platini

Michel Platini did not have an athlete's physique either. In 1972 the club Metz doctor told Platini he was suffering from "a weak heart and poor respiratory capacity." The report was enough for Metz to reject this aspiring player, even though the doctor failed to notice that Platini's ankles were stiff and easily fractured and that he tended to put on weight due to his passion for pasta. In any case, ten years later, shortly before the World Cup in Spain, this defective reject got his revenge: his team, Saint Etienne, beat Metz 9–2.

Platini was the synthesis of the best of French soccer: he had the aim of Justo Fontaine, who in the '58 World Cup scored thirteen goals, a record never beaten, along with the speed and smarts of Raymond Kopa. In each match Platini not only put on a magic show of goals, ones that could not possibly be real, he also lit up the crowd with the way he organized the team's plays. Under his leadership, the French team played a harmonious soccer, fashioned and relished step by step as each play grew organically: precisely the opposite of center to the box, all-out stampede, or God have mercy.

In the semifinals of the '82 World Cup, France lost to Germany in a penalty shootout. That was a duel between Platini and Rummenigge, who was injured but leaped onto the playing field anyway and won the match. Then, in the final, Germany lost to Italy. Neither Platini nor Rummenigge, two players who made soccer history, ever had the pleasure of winning a world championship.

Pagan Sacrifices

In 1985 fanatics of unfortunate renown killed thirty-nine Italian fans on the terraces of the old Heysel Stadium in Brussels. The English club Liverpool was set to play Juventus from Italy in the European Cup final, when hooligans went on the rampage. The Italian fans, cornered against a wall, were trampled among themselves or pushed into an abyss. Television broadcast the butchery live along with the match, which was not suspended.

After that, Italy was off-limits to English fans, even those who carried proof of a good upbringing. In the 1990 World Cup, Italy had no choice but to allow fans onto Sardinia, where the English team was to play, but there were more Scotland Yard agents among them than soccer addicts, and the British minister of sport personally took charge of keeping an eye on them.

One century earlier, in 1890, the *Times* of London had warned: "Our 'Hooligans' go from bad to worse . . . the worse circumstance is that they multiply . . . the 'Hooligan' is a hideous excrescence on our civilization." Today, such excrescence continues to perpetrate crimes under the pretext of soccer.

Wherever hooligans appear, they sow panic. Their bodies are plastered with tattoos on the outside and alcohol on the inside. Patriotic odds and ends hang from their necks and ears, they use brass knuckles and truncheons, and they sweat oceans of violence while howling "Rule Britannia" and other rancorous cheers from the lost empire. In England and in other countries, these thugs also frequently brandish Nazi symbols and proclaim their hatred of blacks, Arabs, Turks, Pakistanis, or Jews.

"Go back to Africa!" roared one Real Madrid "ultra," who enjoyed shouting insults at blacks, "because they've come to take away my job."

Under the pretext of soccer, Italian "Naziskins" whistle at black players and call the enemy fans "Jews": "*Ebrei!*" they shout.

Rowdy crowds that insult soccer the way drunks insult wine are sadly not exclusive to Europe. Nearly every country suffers from them, some more, some less, and over time the rabid dogs have multiplied. Until a few years ago, Chile had the friendliest fans I'd ever seen: men, and women and children too, who held singing contests in the stands that even had judges. Today the

Chilean club Colo-Colo has its own gang of troublemakers, "The White Claw," and the gang from the University of Chile team is called "The Underdogs."

In 1993 Jorge Valdano calculated that during the previous fifteen years more than a hundred people had been killed by violence in Argentina's stadiums. Violence, Valdano said, grows in direct proportion to social injustice and the frustrations that people face in their daily lives. Everywhere, gangs of hooligans attract young people tormented by lack of jobs and lack of hope. A few months after he said this, Boca Juniors from Buenos Aires was defeated 2–0 by River Plate, their traditional rival. Two River fans were shot dead as they left the stadium. "We tied 2–2," commented a young Boca fan interviewed on TV.

In a column he wrote in other times about other sports, Dio Chrysostom painted a portrait of Roman fans of the second century: "When they go to the stadium, it's as if they had discovered a cache of drugs. They forget themselves entirely and without a drop of shame they say and do the first thing that comes into their heads." The worst catastrophe in the history of sport occurred there, in Rome, four centuries later. In the year 512, thousands died—they say thirty thousand, though it's hard to believe—in a street war between two groups of chariot-racing fans that lasted several days.

In soccer stadiums, the tragedy with the most victims occurred in 1964 in the capital of Peru. When the referee disallowed a goal in the final minutes of a match against Argentina, oranges, beer cans, and other projectiles rained down from the stands burning with rage. The police responded with tear gas and bullets, and provoked a stampede. A police charge crushed the crowd against the exit gates, which were closed. More than three hundred died. That night a multitude protested in the streets of Lima: against the referee, not the police.

The 1986 World Cup

Baby Doc Duvalier was fleeing Haiti, taking everything with him. Also stealing and fleeing was Ferdinand Marcos of the Philippines, while US sources revealed (better late than never) that this much-praised Philippine hero of World War II had actually been a deserter.

Halley's Comet was visiting our skies after a long absence, nine moons were being discovered around the planet Uranus, and the first hole was appearing in the ozone layer that protects us from the sun. A new antileukemia drug was being released, the daughter of genetic engineering. In Japan a popular singer was committing suicide and, following her, twenty-three of her fans were choosing death. An earthquake was leaving 200,000 Salvadorans homeless, and a catastrophe at the Soviet nuclear plant in Chernobyl was unleashing a rainstorm of radioactive poison, impossible to measure or to stop, over who-knows-how-many miles and people.

Felipe González was saying *sí* to NATO, the Atlantic military alliance, after having screamed *no*, and a plebiscite was blessing his about-face, while Spain and Portugal were entering the European Common Market. The world was mourning the death of Olof Palme, Sweden's prime minister, assassinated in the street. A time of mourning for the arts and letters: among those taking their leave were sculptor Henry Moore and writers Simone de Beauvoir, Jean Genet, Juan Rulfo, and Jorge Luis Borges.

The Irangate scandal was exploding, implicating President Reagan, the CIA, and Nicaraguan *contras* in gunrunning and drug trafficking, and exploding as well was the spaceship *Challenger*, on takeoff from Cape Canaveral with seven crew members on board. The US Air Force was bombing Libya and killing a daughter of Colonel Gaddafi to punish him for an attack that years later was found to have been perpetrated by Iran.

In a Lima jail, four hundred prisoners were being shot. Well-informed sources in Miami were announcing the imminent fall of Fidel Castro, it was only a matter of hours. Many buildings without proper foundations but with lots of people inside had collapsed when an earthquake struck Mexico City a year before, and a good part of the city was still in ruins when the thirteenth World Cup got under way there.

Participating were fourteen European countries and six from the Americas, as well as Morocco, South Korea, Iraq, and Algeria. "The wave" was born in the stands at the Cup in Mexico, and ever since it has moved fans the world over to the rhythm of a rough sea. There were matches that made your hair stand on end, like France against Brazil where the infallible Platini, Zico, and Sócrates failed on penalty kicks. And there were two spectacular goal fests involving Denmark: they scored six on Uruguay and suffered five scored by Spain.

But this was Maradona's World Cup. With two lefty goals against England, Maradona avenged the wound to his country's pride inflicted in the Falklands war: the first he converted with his left hand, which he called "the hand of God," and the other with his left foot, after having sent the English defenders to the ground.

Argentina faced Germany in the final. It was Maradona who made the decisive pass that left Burruchaga alone with the ball when the clock was running out, so that Argentina could win 3–2 and take the championship. But before that another memorable goal had occurred: Valdano set off with the ball from the Argentine goal and crossed the entire field. When Schumacher came out to meet him, he bounced the ball off the right post and into the net. Valdano talked to the ball as he came upfield, begging her: "Please, go in."

France took third place, followed by Belgium. Lineker of England led the list of scorers with six. Maradona scored five goals, as did Careca of Brazil and Butragueño of Spain.

The Telecracy

Nowadays the stadium is a gigantic TV studio. The game is played for television, so you can watch it at home. And television rules.

At the '86 World Cup, Valdano, Maradona, and other players protested because the important matches were played at noon under a sun that fried everything it touched. Noon in Mexico, nightfall in Europe, that was the best time for European television. The German goalkeeper, Harald Schumacher, told the story: "I sweat. My throat is dry. The grass is like dried shit: hard, strange, hostile. The sun shines straight down on the stadium and strikes us right on the head. We cast no shadows. They say this is good for television."

Was the sale of the spectacle more important than the quality of play? The players are there to kick not to cry, and Havelange put an end to that maddening business: "They should play and shut their traps," he decreed.

Who ran the 1986 World Cup? The Mexican Soccer Federation? No, please, no more intermediaries: it was run by Guillermo

Cañedo, vice president of Televisa and president of the company's international network. This World Cup belonged to Televisa, the private monopoly that owns the free time of all Mexicans and also owns Mexican soccer. And nothing could be more important than the money Televisa, along with FIFA, could earn from the European broadcast rights. When a Mexican journalist had the insolent audacity to ask about the costs and profits of the World Cup, Cañedo cut him off cold: "This is a private company and we don't have to report to anybody."

When the World Cup ended, Cañedo continued as a Havelange courtier occupying one of the vice presidencies of FIFA, another private company that does not have to report to anybody.

Televisa not only holds the reins on national and international broadcasts of Mexican soccer, it also owns three first-division clubs: América, the most powerful, Necaxa, and Atlante.

In 1990 Televisa demonstrated the ferocious power it holds over the Mexican game. That year, the president of the club Puebla, Emilio Maurer, had a deadly idea: Televisa could easily put out more money for the exclusive rights to broadcast the matches. Maurer's initiative was well received by several leaders of the Mexican Soccer Federation. After all, the monopoly paid each club a little more than a thousand dollars, while amassing a fortune from selling advertising.

Televisa then showed them who was boss. Maurer was bombarded without mercy: overnight, creditors foreclosed on his companies and his home, he was threatened, assaulted, and declared a fugitive from justice, and a warrant was issued for his arrest. What's more, one nasty morning his club's stadium was closed without warning. But gangster tactics were not enough to make him climb down from his horse, so they had no choice but to put Maurer in jail and sweep him out of his rebel club and out of the Mexican Soccer Association, along with all of his allies.

Throughout the world, by direct and indirect means, television decides where, when, and how soccer will be played. The game has sold out to the small screen in body and soul and clothing too. Players are now TV stars. Who can compete with their shows? The program that had the largest audience in France and Italy in 1993 was the final of the European Cup Winners' Cup between Olympique de Marseille and AC Milan. Milan, as we all know, belongs to Silvio Berlusconi, the czar of Italian television. Bernard Tapie was not the owner of French TV, but his club, Olympique, received from the small screen that year three hundred times more money than in 1980. He lacked no motive for affection.

Now millions of people can watch matches, not only the thousands who fit into the stadiums. The number of fans has multiplied, along with the number of potential consumers of as many things as the image manipulators wish to sell. But unlike baseball and basketball, soccer is a game of continuous play that offers few interruptions for showing ads. The one halftime is not enough. American television has proposed to correct this unpleasant defect by dividing the matches into four twenty-five-minute periods—and Havelange agrees.

Staid and Standardized

D on Howe, coach of the English team, said in 1987: "A player who feels satisfied after losing a match could never be any good at soccer."

Professional soccer, ever more rapid, ever less beautiful, has tended to become a game of speed and strength, fueled by the fear of losing.

Players run a lot and risk little or nothing. Audacity is not profitable. Over forty years, between the '54 and '94 World Cups, the average number of goals fell by half, even though as of 1994 an extra point was awarded for each victory to try to discourage ties. The highly praised efficiency of mediocrity: in modern soccer ever more teams are made up of functionaries who specialize in avoiding defeat, rather than players who run the risk of acting on inspiration and who allow their creative spirit to take charge.

The Chilean player Carlos Caszely made fun of greedy soccer: "It's the tactic of the bat," he said. "All eleven players hanging from the crossbar."

And the Russian player Nikolai Starostin complained about remote-control soccer: "Now all the players look alike. If they changed shirts, no one would notice. They all play alike."

Playing a staid and standardized soccer, is that really playing? According to those who understand the root meaning of words, "to play" is to joke, and "health" is when the body is as free as can be. The controlled effectiveness of mechanical repetition, enemy of health, is making soccer sick.

To win without magic, without surprise or beauty, isn't that worse than losing? In 1994, during the Spanish championship, Real Madrid was defeated by Sporting from Gijón. But the men of Real Madrid played with enthusiasm, a word that originally meant "having the gods within." The coach, Jorge Valdano, beamed at the players in the dressing room: "When you play like that," he told them, "it's okay to lose."

Running Drugstores

In the '54 World Cup, when Germany burst out with such astonishing speed the Hungarians were left in the gutter, Ferenc Puskás said the German dressing room smelled like a garden of poppies. He claimed that had something to do with the fact that the winners ran like trains.

In 1987 Harald "Toni" Schumacher, the goalkeeper for the German national team, published a book in which he said: "There are too many drugs and not enough women," referring to German soccer and, by extension, to all professional teams. In his book *Der Anpfiff* (The Starting Whistle), Schumacher recounts that at the 1986 World Cup the German players were given innumerable injections and pills and large doses of a mysterious mineral water that gave them diarrhea. Did that team represent Germany or the German chemical industry? The players were even forced to take sleeping pills. Schumacher spat them out; to help him sleep he preferred beer.

The keeper confirmed that the consumption of anabolic steroids and stimulants is common in the professional game. Pressed by the law of productivity to win by any means necessary, many anxious and anguished players become running drugstores. And the same system that condemns them to that also condemns them *for* that every time they get caught.

Schumacher, who admitted that he too took drugs on occasion, was accused of treason. This popular idol, runner-up in two world championships, was knocked from his pedestal and dragged through the mud. Booted off his team, Cologne, he also lost his spot on the national squad and had no choice but to go and play in Turkey.

Chants of Scorn

It's not on any map but it's there. It's invisible, but there it is. A barrier that makes the memory of the Berlin Wall look ridiculous: raised to separate those who have from those who need, it divides the globe into north and south, and draws borders within each country and within each city. When the south of the world commits the affront of scaling the walls and venturing where it shouldn't, the north reminds it, with truncheons, of its proper place. And the same thing happens to those who attempt to leave the zones of the damned in each country and each city.

Soccer, mirror of everything, reflects this reality. In the middle of the 1980s, when Napoli started playing the best soccer in Italy thanks to the magical influx of Maradona, fans in the north of the country reacted by unsheathing the old weapons of scorn. Neapolitans, usurpers of prohibited glory, were snatching trophies from the ever powerful, and it was time to punish the insolence of the intruding scum from the south. In the stadiums of Milan and Turin, banners insulted: "Neapolitans, welcome to Italy." Or they evoked cruelty: "Vesuvius, we're counting on you."

And chants that were the children of fear and the grandchildren of racism resounded more loudly than ever:

> *What a stench, the dogs are running,*
> *all because the Neapolitans are coming.*
> *Oh cholerics buried by quake,*
> *you've never seen soap, not even a cake,*
> *Naples shit, Naples cholera,*
> *you're the shame of all Italia.*

In Argentina the same thing happens to Boca Juniors. Boca is the favorite of the spiky-haired, dark-skinned poor who have invaded the lordly city of Buenos Aires from the scrubby hinterlands and from neighboring countries. The enemy fans exorcise this fearful demon:

> *Boca's in mourning, everybody knows,*
> *'cause they're all black, they're all homos.*
> *Kill the shit-kickers,*
> *they aren't straight.*
> *Throw the bumpkins in the River Plate.*

Anything Goes

In 1988 Mexican journalist Miguel Ángel Ramírez discovered a fountain of youth. Several players on Mexico's junior team, who were two, three, and even six years beyond the age limit, had been bathed in the magic waters: the directors falsified their birth certificates and fabricated fake passports. This treatment was so effective that one player managed to become two years younger than his twin brother.

Then the vice president of Guadalajara declared: "I won't say it's a good thing, but it's always been done."

And Rafael del Castillo, who was the top boss of junior soccer, asked: "Why can't Mexico be sneaky when other countries do it as a matter of course?"

⊚ ⊚ ⊚ ⊚ ⊚ ⊚ ⊚ ⊚ ⊚ ⊚ ⊚ ⊚ ⊚ ⊚

Shortly after the 1966 World Cup the comptroller of the Argentine Soccer Association, Valentín Suárez, declared: "Stanley Rous is a shady fellow. He ran the World Cup so that England would win. I'd do the same if the Cup were played in Argentina."

The morals of the market, which in our days are the morals of the world, give a green light to all keys to success, even if they're burglar's tools. Professional soccer has no scruples because it is part of an unscrupulous system of power that buys effectiveness at any price. And after all, scruples were never worth much. In Renaissance Italy a "scruple" was the smallest measure of weight, the least significant. Five centuries later, Paul Steiner, a player for the German club Cologne, explained: "I play for money and for points. The opposing player wants to take my money and my points. That's why I ought to fight him by all means at my disposal."

And the Dutch player Ronald Koeman justified the brutal kick to the stomach his compatriot Gillhaus gave the Frenchman Tigana in 1988: "It was a class act. Tigana was their most dangerous player and he had to be neutralized at any cost."

The end justifies the means, and any beastly act is fine, though it's wise to do it on the sly. Basile Boli of Olympique de Marseille, a defender accused of mistreating the ankles of others, described his baptism by fire. In 1983 Roger Milla was elbowing him like crazy, so he flattened him with his head. "That was the first lesson: strike before they strike you, but strike discreetly."

You have to strike far from the ball, since that is where the referee, like the TV cameras, keeps his eyes. In the 1970 World Cup Pelé was marked savagely by the Italian Bertini. Later on he praised him: "Bertini was an artist at committing fouls without being seen. He'd punch me in the ribs or in the stomach, he'd kick me in the ankle . . . An artist."

Argentine journalists frequently applaud the wiles of Carlos Bilardo because he knows how to deploy them carefully and effectively. They say that when Bilardo was a player he would prick his opponents with a pin and put on an innocent face. And when he was manager of the Argentine national team, he managed to send a canteen filled with emetic water to Branco, a thirsty Brazilian player, during the toughest match of the 1990 World Cup.

Uruguayan journalists like to call brazen crime a "strong-legged play," and more than one has celebrated the effectiveness of the "softening kick" to intimidate opposing players in international contests. That kick must be given in the first minutes of the match. Later on, you run the risk of being sent off. In Uruguayan soccer, violence is the daughter of decadence. Long ago, "Charrua's claw" was a term for bravery, not for a vicious kick.

In the 1950 World Cup, during the famous final in Maracaná, Brazil committed twice as many fouls as Uruguay. In the 1990 Cup, when the manager Oscar Tabárez managed to get the Uruguayan team to go back to playing cleanly, several local commentators took pleasure in affirming that it did not achieve much. There are many fans and officials, too, who prefer winning without honor to losing nobly.

Uruguayan forward "Pepe" Sasía said: "Throw dirt in the eyes of the goalkeeper? Managers don't like it when you get caught."

Argentine fans heap praise on the goal that Maradona scored with his hand in the '86 World Cup, *because the referee didn't see it.* In the qualifiers for the World Cup in 1990, Chile's keeper Roberto Rojas pretended to be wounded by cutting himself on the forehead, but he got caught. Chile's fans, who adored Rojas and called him "The Condor," suddenly turned him into the villain of the picture, *because his ploy didn't work.*

In professional soccer, like everything else, the crime does not matter as long as the alibi is good. "Culture" means cultivation. What does the culture of power cultivate in us? What sad harvests could come of a power that bestows impunity on the crimes of the military and the graft of politicians and converts them into triumphs?

The writer Albert Camus, who once was a goalkeeper in Algeria, was not referring to the professional game when he said: "Everything I know about morals, I owe to soccer."

Indigestion

In 1989 in Buenos Aires, a match between Argentinos Juniors and Racing ended in a draw. The rules called for a penalty shootout.

The crowd was on its feet, biting its nails, for the first shots at twelve paces. The fans cheered a goal by Racing. Then came a goal by Argentinos Juniors and the fans from the other side cheered. There was an ovation when the Racing keeper leaped against one post and sent the ball awry. Another ovation praised the Argentinos keeper who did not allow himself to be seduced by the expression on the striker's face and waited for the ball in the center of the goal.

When the tenth penalty was kicked, there was another round of applause. A few fans left the stadium after the twentieth. When the thirtieth penalty came around, the few who remained responded with yawns. Kicks came and went and the match remained tied.

After forty-four penalty kicks, the match ended. It was a world record for penalties. In the stadium no one was left to celebrate, and no one even knew which side won.

The 1990 World Cup

Nelson Mandela was free, after spending twenty-seven years in prison for being black and proud in South Africa. In Colombia the left's presidential candidate, Bernardo Jaramillo, lay dying and from a helicopter the police were shooting drug trafficker Rodríguez Gacha, one of the ten richest men in the world. Chile's badly wounded democracy was recuperating, but General Pinochet, at the head of the military, was still keeping an eye on the politicians and reining in their every step. Alberto Fujimori, riding a tractor, was beating Mario Vargas Llosa in the Peruvian elections. In Nicaragua, the Sandinistas were losing that country's elections, defeated by the exhaustion wrought by ten years of war against invaders armed and trained by the United States, while the United States was beginning a new occupation of Panama following the success of its twenty-first invasion of that country.

In Poland labor leader Lech Walesa, a man of daily mass, was exiting jail and entering government. In Moscow a crowd was lining up at McDonald's. The Berlin Wall was being sold off in pieces, as the unification of the two Germanys and the disintegration of Yugoslavia began. A popular insurrection was putting an end to the Ceausescu regime in Romania, and the veteran dictator, who liked to call himself the "Blue Danube of Socialism," was being executed. In all of Eastern Europe, old bureaucrats were turning into new entrepreneurs and cranes were dragging off statues of Marx, who had no way of saying, "I'm innocent." Well-informed sources in Miami were announcing the imminent fall of Fidel Castro, it was only a matter of hours. Up in heaven, terrestrial machines were visiting Venus and spying on its secrets, while here on earth, in Italy, the fourteenth World Cup got under way.

Fourteen teams from Europe and six from the Americas took part, plus Egypt, South Korea, the United Arab Emirates, and Cameroon, which astonished the world by defeating the Argentine side in the first match and then playing head to head with England. Roger Milla, a forty-year-old veteran, was first drum in this African orchestra.

Maradona, with one foot swelled up like a pumpkin, did the best he could to lead his team. You could barely hear the tango. After losing to Cameroon, Argentina drew with Romania and Italy and was about to lose to Brazil. The Brazilians dominated the entire match, until Maradona, playing on one leg, evaded three markers at midfield and set up Caniggia, who scored before you could even exhale.

Argentina faced Germany in the final, just as in the previous Cup, but this time Germany won 1–0 thanks to an invisible foul and Beckenbauer's wise coaching.

Italy took third place, England fourth. Schillaci of Italy led the list of scorers with six, followed by Skuharavy of Czechoslovakia with five. This championship, boring soccer without a drop of audacity or beauty, had the lowest average scores in World Cup history.

Goal by Rincón

I t happened at the World Cup in 1990. Colombia was playing better than Germany, but was losing the match 1–0.

Then, in the final minute, the ball reached midfield in search of a head with an electrified afro: Valderrama got the ball from behind, turned, shook off three Germans he had no need of, and passed to Rincón. The ball traveled from Rincón to Valderrama, Valderrama to Rincón, yours and mine, mine and yours, touch after touch, until Rincón loped forward several paces like a giraffe and faced Illgner, the German keeper, alone. Illgner covered the goal completely. So Rincón didn't kick the ball, he caressed her. And she slid softly between the goalkeeper's legs and scored.

Hugo Sánchez

As 1992 unfolded, Yugoslavia fell to pieces. War taught brothers to hate each other, and to kill and rape without remorse.

Two Mexican journalists, Epi Ibarra and Hernán Vera, wanted to go to Sarajevo. Bombarded, under siege, Sarajevo was off-limits to the foreign press, and recklessness had already cost more than one reporter his life.

Chaos reigned on all approaches to the city. Everyone against everyone else: no one was sure who was who, or who they were fighting in that bedlam of trenches, smoking ruins, and unburied bodies. Map in hand, Epi and Hernán made their way through the thunder of artillery fire and machine-gun blasts, until on the banks of the Drina River they suddenly came face-to-face with a large group of soldiers who threw them to the ground and took aim at their chests. The officer bellowed who knows what and the reporters mumbled back who knows what else. But when the officer drew his finger across his throat and the rifles went click, they understood that there was nothing left to do but say good-bye and pray, just in case there is a heaven.

Then it occurred to the condemned men to show their passports. The officer's face lit up. "Mexico!" he screamed. "Hugo Sánchez!"

And he dropped his weapon and hugged them.

Hugo Sánchez, the Mexican key to impossible locks, became world famous thanks to television, which showcased the art of his goals and the handsprings he turned to celebrate them. In the 1989–1990 season, wearing the uniform of Real Madrid, he burst the nets thirty-eight times and became the leading foreign scorer in the entire history of Spanish soccer.

The Cricket and the Ant

In 1992 the singing cricket defeated the worker ant 2–0.

Germany and Denmark faced each other in the final of the European Championship. The German players were raised on fasting, abstinence, and hard work, the Danes on beer, women, and naps in the sun. Denmark had lost out in the qualifiers and the players were on vacation when war intervened and they got an urgent call to take Yugoslavia's place in the tournament. They had no time for training nor any interest in it, and had to make do without their most brilliant star, Michael Laudrup, a sure-footed player who had just won the European Cup wearing a Barcelona shirt. The German team, on the other hand, came to the final with Matthäus, Klinsmann, and all of its other big guns. Germany, which should have won, was defeated by Denmark, which had nothing to prove and played as if the field were a continuation of the beach.

Gullit

In 1993 a tide of racism was rising. Its stench, like a recurring nightmare, already hung over Europe; several crimes were committed and laws to keep out ex-colonial immigrants were passed. Many young whites, unable to find work, began to blame their plight on people with dark skin.

That year a team from France won the European Cup for the first time. The winning goal was the work of Basile Boli, an African from the Ivory Coast, who headed in a corner kicked by another African, Abedi Pele, who was born in Ghana. Meanwhile, not even the blindest proponents of white supremacy could deny that the Netherlands' best players were the veterans Ruud Gullit and Frank Rijkaard, dark-skinned sons of Surinamese parents, or that the African Eusébio had been Portugal's best soccer player ever.

Ruud Gullit, known as "The Black Tulip," had always been a full-throated opponent of racism. Guitar in hand, he sang at anti-apartheid concerts between matches, and in 1987, when he was chosen Europe's most valuable player, he dedicated his Ballon d'Or to Nelson Mandela, who spent many years in jail for the crime of believing that blacks are human.

One of Gullit's knees was operated on three times. Each time commentators declared he was finished. Out of sheer desire he always came back: "When I can't play I'm like a newborn with nothing to suck."

His nimble scoring legs and his imposing stature crowned by a head of Rasta dreadlocks won him a fervent following when he played for the strongest teams in the Netherlands and Italy. But Gullit never got along with coaches or managers because he tended to disobey orders, and he had the stubborn habit of speaking out against the culture of money that is reducing soccer to just another listing on the stock exchange.

Parricide

At the end of the southern winter of 1993, Colombia's national team played a World Cup qualifier in Buenos Aires. When the Colombian players took the field, they were greeted with a shower of whistles, boos, and insults. When they left, the crowd gave them a standing ovation that echoes to this day.

Argentina lost 5–0. As usual, the goalkeeper carried the cross of the defeat, but this time the visitors' victory was celebrated as never before. To a one, the fans cheered the Colombians' incredible style, a feast of legs, a joy for the eyes, an ever-changing dance that invented its own music as the match progressed. The lordly play of "El Pibe" Balderrama, a working-class mulatto, was the envy of princes, and the black players were the kings of this carnival: not a soul could get past Perea or stop "Freight Train" Valencia; not a soul could deal with the tentacles of "Octopus" Asprilla or block the bullets fired by Rincón. Given the color of their skin and the intensity of their joy, those Colombians looked like Brazil in its glory years.

The Colombian press called the massacre a "parricide." Half a century before, the founding fathers of soccer in Bogotá, Medellín, and Cali were Argentines. But life has its surprises: Pedernera, Di Stéfano, Rossi, Rial, Pontoni, and Moreno fathered a child who turned out to be Brazilian.

Goal by Zico

I t was 1993. In Tokyo, Kashima was playing Tohoku for the Emperor's Cup.

The Brazilian Zico, star of Kashima, scored the winning goal, the loveliest of his career. The ball reached the center on a cross from the right. Zico, who was in the semicircle, leaped forward. But he jumped too soon. When he realized the ball was behind him, he turned a somersault in midair and with his face to the ground he drove it in with his heel. It was a backward overhead volley.

"Tell me about that goal," plead the blind.

A Sport of Evasion

When Spain was still suffering under the Franco dictatorship, Real Madrid president Santiago Bernabéu set out a definition of the club's mission: "We are serving the nation. What we want is to make people happy."

His colleague from Atlético de Madrid, Vicente Calderón, also praised the sport's virtue as a collective Valium: "Soccer keeps people from thinking about more dangerous things."

In 1993 and 1994 the directors of several soccer teams around the world were charged and prosecuted for swindles of various sorts. Evidently soccer is useful not only for hiding social tensions and evading social conflict, but also for hiding assets and evading taxes.

The days are long gone when the most important clubs in the world belonged to the fans and the players. In those remote times, the club president went around with a bucket of lime and a brush to paint the lines on the field, and as for directors, their most extravagant act was footing the bill for a celebratory feast in the neighborhood pub. Today clubs are corporations that move fortunes to hire players and sell spectacles, and they have grown accustomed to tricking the state, fooling the public, and violating labor rights and every other right. They are also used to impunity. There is no multinational corporation that enjoys greater impunity than FIFA, the association of professional clubs. FIFA has its own justice system. Like the Queen of Hearts in *Alice in Wonderland*,

FIFA's unjust system sentences first and tries later, so there will be plenty of time to cover up.

Professional soccer operates at the margins of the law, in a sacred territory where it can dictate its own laws and ignore all others. But why should the law operate at the margins of soccer? Judges rarely dare to red-card the big clubs for cooking the books to score illegal goals on the public treasury and leave the rules of clean play sprawled on the ground. The fact is judges know they risk a sharp whistle if they use an iron hand. Professional soccer is untouchable because it is popular. "The directors steal for us," say the fans, and they believe it.

Some judges are prepared to defy the tradition of impunity, and recent scandals have shone a little light on the financial acrobatics and shell games that some of the richest clubs in the world play as a matter of course.

When the president of the Italian club Perugia was accused of buying referees in 1993, he counterattacked by charging, "Eighty percent of soccer is corrupt."

Experts agree he was being generous. Every important club in Italy, from north to south, from Milan and Torino to Napoli and Cagliari, is involved in fraud, some more, some less. Their falsified balance sheets hide debts several times the value of their capital; the directors maintain slush funds, phantom companies, and secret Swiss accounts; instead of taxes and social security they pay hefty bills for services not rendered; and the players tend to pocket a lot less money than the books say they receive, as it gets lost along the way.

The same tricks are common among the most well-known clubs of France. Several directors of Bordeaux were charged with embezzling funds for personal use, and the head honchos of Olympique de Marseille were taken to court for bribing their opponents. Olympique, the most powerful club in France, was knocked down to second division and lost the titles of champion of France and champion of Europe when its directors were caught bribing several players from Valenciennes just before a match in 1993. That episode put an end to the sporting career and political ambitions of the businessman Bernard Tapie, who got a year in prison and ended up bankrupt.

At the same time, the Polish champion Club Legia lost its title for having "arranged" two matches, and Tottenham Hotspur in England revealed that it had been asked to make payments under the table to obtain a player from Nottingham Forest. The English club Luton, meanwhile, was being investigated for tax evasion.

Several soccer scandals erupted simultaneously in Brazil. The president of Botafogo charged that the directors of Brazil's professional league had manipulated seven matches in 1993, winning a small fortune in bets. In São Paulo other lawsuits revealed that a local soccer federation boss had grown rich overnight, and when certain phantom accounts were examined it became clear that his sudden fortune did not result from a life devoted to the noble calling of sport. As if that were not enough, the president of the Brazilian Soccer Confederation, Ricardo Teixeira, was sued by Pelé for taking bribes in the sale of television broadcast rights. In response to Pelé's suit, Havelange named Teixeira, who is his son-in-law, to the FIFA board.

Nearly two thousand years before all this, the biblical patriarch who wrote the book of Acts told the story of two early Christians, Ananias and his wife Sapphira, who sold a piece of land and lied about the price. When God found out, he killed them on the spot.

If God had time for soccer, how many directors would remain alive?

The 1994 World Cup

The Mayas of Chiapas were up in arms, the real Mexico blowing up in the face of the official Mexico, and Subcommandante Marcos was astonishing the world with his words of humor and amour.

Onetti, the novelist of the dark side of the soul, lay dying. World car-racing champion Ayrton Senna, a Brazilian, was being decapitated on an unsafe European track. Serbs, Croats, and Muslims were killing each other in the pieces that had been Yugoslavia. In Rwanda something similar was happening, but television spoke of tribes, not peoples, and implied that the violence was the sort of thing black people do.

Torrijos's heirs were winning the Panamanian elections four years after the bloody invasion and useless occupation by the United States. US troops were pulling out of Somalia, where they had fought hunger with bullets. South Africa was voting for Mandela. Communists, rebaptized as socialists, were winning parliamentary elections in Lithuania, Ukraine, Poland, and Hungary, all countries that had discovered that capitalism also has certain inconvenient traits. But Moscow's Progress Publishers, which used to publish the works of Marx and Lenin, was now publishing *Reader's Digest*. Well-informed sources in Miami were announcing the imminent fall of Fidel Castro, it was only a matter of hours.

Corruption scandals were demolishing Italy's political parties and filling the power vacuum was Berlusconi, the parvenu who ran the dictatorship of television in the name of democratic diversity. Berlusconi was crowning his campaign with a slogan stolen from the soccer stadiums, while the fifteenth World Cup got under way in the United States, the home of baseball.

The US press gave the matter scant attention, saying more or less: "Here soccer is the sport of the future and it always will be." But the stadiums were packed despite a sun that melted stones. To please European television, the big matches were played at noon, as in Mexico at the '86 Cup.

Thirteen teams from Europe, six from the Americas, and three from Africa took part, plus South Korea and Saudi Arabia. To discourage ties, three points were given for each win instead of two. And to discourage violence, the referees were much more rigorous than usual, handing out warnings and ejections throughout the tournament. For the first time the referees wore colorful uniforms and for the first time each team was allowed a third substitute to replace an injured goalkeeper.

Maradona played in his final World Cup and it was a party, until he was defeated in the laboratory that tested his urine after the second match. Without him and without the speed demon Caniggia, Argentina fell apart. Nigeria played the most entertaining soccer of the Cup. Bulgaria, Stoichkov's team, won fourth place after knocking the fearful German squad out of the running. Third place went to Sweden. Italy faced Brazil in the final. It was a boring, drawn-out affair that ended scoreless, but between yawns Romário and Baggio offered some lessons in good soccer. In the penalty shootout, Brazil won 3–2 and was crowned champion of the world. An amazing story: Brazil is the only country that qualified for every World Cup, the only country to win it four times, the country that has won the most matches, and the country that has scored the most goals.

Leading the list of scorers in the '94 Cup were Stoichkov of Bulgaria and Salenko of Russia with six goals, followed by Brazil's Romário, Italy's Baggio, Sweden's Andersson, and Germany's Klinsmann, with five apiece.

Romário

From who knows what part of the stratosphere, the tiger appears, mauls, and vanishes. The goalkeeper, trapped in his cage, does not even have time to blink. Romário fires off one goal after another: half-volley, bicycle, on the fly, banana shot, backheel, toe poke, side tap.

Romário was born poor in a favela called Jacarezinho, but even as a child he practiced writing his name to prepare for the many autographs he would sign in his life. He clambered up the ladder to fame without paying the toll of obligatory lies: this very poor man always enjoyed the luxury of doing whatever he wished, a barhopping lover of the night who always said what he thought without thinking about what he was saying.

Now he owns a collection of Mercedes-Benz cars and 250 pairs of shoes, but his best friends are still that bunch of unpresentable hustlers who, in his childhood, taught him how to make the kill.

Baggio

In recent years no one has given Italians better soccer or more to talk about. Roberto Baggio's game is mysterious: his legs have a mind of their own, his foot shoots by itself, his eyes see the goals before they happen.

Baggio is a big horsetail that flicks away opponents as he flows forward in an elegant wave. Opponents harass him, they bite, they punch him hard. Baggio has Buddhist sayings written under his captain's armband. Buddha does not ward off the blows, but he does help suffer them. From his infinite serenity, he also helps Baggio discover the silence that lies beyond the din of cheers and whistles.

A Few Numbers

Between 1930 and 1994 the Americas won eight World Cups and Europe won seven. Brazil won the trophy four times, Argentina twice, and Uruguay twice. Italy and Germany were world champions three times apiece; England only won the Cup played on its home turf.

However, since Europe's teams formed the overwhelming majority, it had twice as many chances. In fifteen World Cups, European teams had 159 opportunities to win, compared with only seventy-seven opportunities for teams from the Americas. What's more, the overwhelming majority of the referees have been European.

Unlike the World Cup, the Intercontinental Cup has offered the same number of opportunities to the teams of Europe and the Americas. In these tournaments, waged by clubs rather than national teams, squads from the Americas have won twenty times to the Europeans' thirteen.

The case of Great Britain is the most astonishing in this matter of inequality of rights in world soccer championships. The way they explained it to me as a child, God is one but He's three: Father, Son, and Holy Ghost. I never could understand it. And I still don't understand why Great Britain is one but she's four: England, Scotland, Northern Ireland, and Wales, while Spain and Switzerland, to take two examples, continue to be no more than one despite the diverse nationalities that make them up.

In any case, Europe's traditional control is beginning to break down. Until the 1994 World Cup, FIFA accepted one or two token countries from the rest of the world, as if paying a tax to the *mappa mundi*. Starting with the '98 Cup, the number of participating countries will go from twenty-four to thirty-two. Europe will maintain its unjust proportion in relation to the Americas, but it will have to contend with greater participation by the countries of black Africa, with their lightning and joyful soccer in full expansion, and also Arab and Asian countries, like the Chinese who pioneered the sport but until now have had to watch from the stands.

[Since this was written in 1995, Europe has won three more championships and the Americas one, giving Europe a 10–9 edge overall. Brazil has now won the trophy an astounding five times, Italy four. But geographical injustice persists: FIFA continues to allot three times as many berths to Europe as to the Americas. In 2014, the thirty-two contenders that meet in Brazil will feature thirteen from Europe, four or five from South America, five from Africa, four or five from Asia, three or four from North and Central America plus the Caribbean, and, if lucky, one will travel all the way from Oceania.]

The Duty of Losing

For Bolivia, qualifying for the '94 World Cup was like reaching the moon. Penned in by geography and mistreated by history, it had attended other World Cups only by invitation and had lost all its matches, failing to score a single goal.

The work of manager Xabier Azkargorta was paying off, not only in La Paz where you play above the clouds, but at sea level. Bolivia was proving that altitude was not its only great player; the team could overcome the hang-ups that obliged it to lose before the match even began. Bolivia sparkled in the qualifying rounds. Melgar and Baldivieso in the midfield and the forwards Sánchez and above all Etcheverry, known as "El Diablo," were cheered by the most demanding of crowds.

As bad luck would have it, Bolivia had to open the World Cup against all-powerful Germany. A baby finger against Rambo. But no one could have foreseen the outcome: instead of shrinking back into the box, Bolivia went on the attack. They didn't play equal against equal. No, they played as the big guys against the little. Germany, thrown off stride, was in flight and Bolivia was in ecstasy. And that's how it continued, until the moment when Bolivia's star Marco Antonio Etcheverry took the field only to kick Matthäus inexcusably and get sent off. Then the Bolivians collapsed, wishing they had never sinned against the secret spell cast from the depths of centuries that obliges them to lose.

The Sin of Losing

Soccer elevates its divinities and exposes them to the vengeance of the believers. With ball on his foot and the national colors on his chest, the player who embodies the nation marches off to win glory on far-off battlefields. If he returns in defeat, the warrior becomes a fallen angel. At Ezeiza airport in 1958, people threw coins at Argentina's players returning from a poor performance at the World Cup in Sweden. At the '82 Cup, Caszely missed a penalty kick and in Chile they made his life impossible. Ten years later, several Ethiopian players asked the United Nations for asylum after losing 6–1 to Egypt.

We are because we win. If we lose, we no longer exist. Without question, the national uniform has become the clearest symbol of collective identity, not only in poor or small countries whose place on the map depends on soccer. When England lost out in the qualifiers for the 1994 World Cup, the front page of London's *Daily Mirror* featured a headline in a type size fit for a catastrophe: "THE END OF THE WORLD."

In soccer, as in everything else, losing is not allowed. In these end of century days, failure is the only sin that cannot be redeemed. During the '94 Cup a handful of fanatics burned down the home of Joseph Bell, the defeated Cameroon goalkeeper, and shortly after Colombian player Andrés Escobar was gunned down in Medellín. Escobar had had the bad luck of scoring an own goal, an unforgivable act of treason.

Should we blame soccer? Or should we blame the culture of success and the whole system of power that professional soccer reflects? Soccer is not by nature a violent sport, although at times it becomes a vehicle for letting off steam. It was no coincidence that the murder of Escobar took place in one of the most violent countries on the planet. Violence is not in the genes of these people who love to party and are wild about the joys of music and soccer. Colombians suffer from violence like a disease, but they do not wear it like a birthmark on their foreheads. The machinery of power, on the other hand, is indeed a cause of violence. As in all of Latin America, injustice and humiliation poison people's souls under a tradition of impunity that rewards the unscrupulous, encourages crime, and helps to perpetuate it as a national trait.

A few months before the '94 Cup began, Amnesty International published a report according to which hundreds of Colombians "were executed without due process by the armed forces and their paramilitary allies in 1993. Most of the victims of these extrajudicial executions were people without known political affiliation."

The Amnesty report also exposed the role of the Colombian police in "social cleanup" operations, a euphemism for the systematic extermination of homosexuals, prostitutes, drug addicts, beggars, the mentally ill, and street children. Society calls them "disposables," human garbage that ought to die.

In this world that punishes failure, they are the perennial losers.

Maradona

He played, he won; he peed, he lost. Ephedrine turned up in his urinalysis and Maradona was booted out of the 1994 World Cup. Ephedrine, though not considered a stimulant by professional sports in the United States or many other countries, is prohibited in international competitions.

There was stupefaction and scandal, a blast of moral condemnation that left the whole world deaf. But somehow a few voices of support for the fallen idol managed to squeak through, not only in his wounded and dumbfounded Argentina, but in places as far away as Bangladesh, where a sizable demonstration repudiating FIFA and demanding Maradona's return shook the streets. After all, to judge and condemn was easy. It was not so easy to forget that for many years Maradona had committed the sin of being the best, the crime of speaking out about things the powerful wanted kept quiet, and the felony of playing left-handed, which according to the *Oxford English Dictionary* means not only "of or pertaining to the left hand" but also "sinister or questionable."

Diego Armando Maradona never used stimulants before matches to stretch the limits of his body. It is true that he was into cocaine, but only at sad parties where he wanted to forget or be forgotten because he was cornered by glory and could not live without the fame that would not allow him to live in peace. He played better than anyone else in spite of the cocaine, not because of it.

He was overwhelmed by the weight of his own personality. Ever since that day long ago when fans first chanted his name, his spinal column caused him grief. Maradona carried a burden named Maradona that bent his back out of shape. The body as metaphor: his legs ached, he couldn't sleep without pills. It did not take him long to realize it was impossible to live with the responsibility of being a god on the field, but from the beginning he knew that stopping was out of the question. "I need them to need me," he confessed after many years of living under the tyrannical halo of superhuman performance, swollen with cortisone and analgesics and praise, harassed by the demands of his devotees and by the hatred of those he offended.

The pleasure of demolishing idols is directly proportional to the need to erect them. In Spain, when Goicoechea hit him from behind—even though he didn't have the ball—and sidelined him for several months, some fanatics carried the author of this premeditated homicide on their shoulders. And all over the world plenty of people were ready to celebrate the fall of that arrogant interloper, that parvenu fugitive from hunger, that greaser who had the insolent audacity to swagger and boast.

Later on in Naples, Maradona was Santa Maradonna, and the patron saint San Gennaro became San Gennarmando. In the streets they sold pictures of this divinity in shorts illuminated by the halo of the Virgin or wrapped in the sacred mantle of the saint who bleeds every six months. They even sold coffins for the clubs of northern Italy and tiny bottles filled with the tears of Silvio Berlusconi. Kids and dogs wore Maradona wigs. Somebody placed a ball under the foot of the statue of Dante, and in the famous fountain Triton wore the blue shirt of Napoli. It had been more than half a century since this city, condemned to suffer the furies of Vesuvius and eternal defeat on the soccer field, had last won a championship, and thanks to Maradona the dark south finally managed to humiliate the white north that scorned it. In the stadiums of Italy and all Europe, Napoli kept on winning, cup after cup, and each goal constituted a desecration of the established order and a revenge against history. In Milan they hated the man responsible for this affront by the uppity poor: they called him "ham with curls." And not only in Milan: at the 1990 World Cup most of the spectators punished Maradona with furious whistles every time he touched the ball, and celebrated Argentina's defeat by Germany as a victory for Italy.

When Maradona said he wanted to leave Naples, some people tossed wax dolls stuck with pins through his window. Prisoner of the city that adored him, and of the Camorra, the Mafia that owns it, he was playing against his heart, against his feet. That's when the cocaine scandal erupted, and Maradona suddenly became Maracoca, a delinquent who had fooled people into thinking he was a hero.

Later on in Buenos Aires the media gave a further twist to the knife: live coverage of his arrest, as if it were a match, to the delight of those who love the spectacle of a king disrobed and carted off by the police.

"He's sick," they said. They said, "He's done for." The Messiah who came to redeem southern Italians from their eternal damnation was also the avenger of Argentina's defeat in the Falklands by means of one sneaky goal and another fabulous one that left the English spinning like tops for several years. But when he fell, the Golden Boy was nothing but a numb-nosed whoring phony. Maradona had betrayed the children who adored him and brought dishonor on the sport. They gave him up for dead.

But the body sat up. Once he had served his cocaine sentence, Maradona became the fireman of the Argentine squad, which was burning up its last chances to reach the '94 World Cup. Thanks to Maradona, they made it. And at the Cup once again, as in the old days, Maradona was the best of the best until the ephedrine scandal hit.

The machinery of power had sworn to get him. He spoke truth to power and you pay a price for that, a price paid in cash with no discount. And Maradona himself gave them the excuse, with his suicidal tendency to serve himself up on a platter to his many enemies and that childish irresponsibility that makes him step in every trap laid in his path.

The same reporters who harass him with their microphones, reproach him for his arrogance and his tantrums, and accuse him of talking too much. They aren't wrong, but that's not why they can't forgive him. What they really cannot stand are the things he sometimes says. This hot-tempered little wiseacre has the habit of throwing uppercuts. In '86 and '94, in Mexico and the United States, he complained about the omnipotent dictatorship of television, which forced the players to work themselves to the bone at noon, roasting under the sun. And on a thousand and one other occasions, throughout the ups and downs of his career, Maradona said things that stirred up the hornet's nest. He wasn't the only disobedient player, but his was the voice that made the most offensive questions ring out loud and clear: Why aren't the international standards for labor rights applied to soccer? If it's standard practice for performers to know how much money their shows bring in, why can't the players have access to the books of the opulent multinational of soccer? Havelange, busy with other duties, kept his mouth shut, while Joseph Blatter, a FIFA bureaucrat who never once kicked a ball but goes about in a twenty-five-foot limousine driven by a black chauffeur, had but one comment: "The last star from Argentina was Di Stéfano."

When Maradona was finally thrown out of the '94 World Cup, soccer lost its most strident rebel. And also a fantastic player. Maradona is uncontrollable when he speaks, but much more so when he plays. No one can predict the devilish tricks this inventor of surprises will dream up for the simple joy of throwing the computers off track, tricks he never repeats. He's not quick, more like a short-legged bull, but he carries the ball sewn to his foot and he has eyes all over his body. His acrobatics light up the field. He can win a match with a thundering blast when his back is to the goal, or with an impossible pass from afar when he is corralled by thousands of enemy legs. And no one can stop him when he decides to dribble upfield.

In the frigid soccer of today's world, which detests defeat and forbids all fun, that man was one of the few who proved that fantasy too can be effective.

They Don't Count

A t the end of 1994, Maradona, Stoichkov, Bebeto, Francescoli, Laudrup, Zamorano, Hugo Sánchez, and other players started organizing an international soccer players union.

Up to now the stars of the show have been blindingly absent from the structures of power where decisions are made. They have no say in the management of local soccer, and neither can they enjoy the luxury of being heard in the heights of FIFA where the global pie is divvied up.

Who are the players? Monkeys in a circus? They may dress in silk, but aren't they still monkeys? They are never consulted when it comes to deciding when, where, and how they play. The international bureaucracy changes the rules at its whim, the players have no say. They can't even find out how much money their legs produce, or where those fugitive fortunes end up.

After many years of strikes and demonstrations by local unions, the players have won better contracts, but the merchants of soccer continue treating them as if they were machines to be bought, sold, and loaned: "Maradona is an investment," the president of Napoli liked to say.

Now European clubs, as well as a few Latin American ones, have psychologists on staff, as in factories. The directors do not pay them to help troubled souls, but to oil the machinery and increase productivity. Athletic productivity? Labor productivity, though in this case the hired hands are really hired feet. The fact is that professional players offer their labor power to the factories of spectacle in exchange for a wage. The price depends on performance, and the more they get paid the more they are expected to produce. Trained to win or to win, squeezed to the last calorie, they are treated worse than racehorses. Racehorses? British player Paul Gascoigne likes to compare himself to a factory-raised chicken: controlled movements, rigid rules, set behaviors that must always be repeated.

Stars can earn top salaries while their fleeting splendor lasts. Clubs pay them much more now than twenty or thirty years ago, and they can sell their names and faces for advertising. But the glorious idols of soccer are not rewarded with the fabled treasure people imagine. *Forbes* magazine published a list of the forty top-earning athletes in the world in 1994. Only one soccer player was among them, the Italian Roberto Baggio, and he fell near the bottom of the list.

What about the thousands upon thousands of players who are not stars? The ones who do not enter the kingdom of fame, who get stuck going round and round in the revolving door? Of every ten professional soccer players in Argentina, only three manage to make a living from it. The salaries are not great, especially considering the short duration of an active player's career: cannibalistic industrial civilization devours them in a flash.

[Four soccer stars kicked their way into Forbes's *top forty in 2012: David Beckham (#8), Cristiano Ronaldo (#9), Lionel Messi (#11) and Wayne Rooney (#38). A few millionaire exceptions that prove the rule.]*

An Export Industry

Here is the itinerary of a player from the southern reaches of the globe who has good legs and good luck. From his hometown he moves to a provincial city, then from the provincial city to a small club in the country's capital. The small club has no choice but to sell him to a large one. The large club, suffocated by debt, sells him to an even larger club in a larger country. And the player crowns his career in Europe.

All along this chain, the clubs, contractors, and intermediaries end up with the lion's share of the money. Each link confirms and perpetuates inequality among the parties, from the hopeless plight of neighborhood clubs in poor countries to the omnipotence of the corporations that run European leagues.

In Uruguay, for example, soccer is an export industry that scorns the domestic market. The continuous outflow of good players means mediocre professional leagues and ever fewer, ever less fervent fans. People desert the stadiums to watch foreign matches on television. When the World Cup comes around, our players come from the four corners of the earth, meet on the plane, play together for a short while, and bid each other goodbye, without ever having time to jell into a real team: eleven heads, twenty-two legs, and a single heart.

When Brazil won its fourth World Cup, only a few of the celebrating journalists managed to hide their nostalgia for the marvels of days past. The team of Romário and Bebeto played an efficient match, but it was stingy on poetry: a soccer much less Brazilian than the hypnotic play of Garrincha, Didi, Pelé, and their teammates in '58, '62, and '70. More than one reporter noted the shortage of talent, and several commentators pointed to the style of play imposed by the manager, successful but lacking in magic: Brazil had sold its soul to modern soccer. But there was another point that went practically unmentioned: the great teams of the past were made up of Brazilians who played in Brazil. On the 1994 team, eight of them played in Europe. Romario, the highest-paid Latin American player in the world, was earning more in Spain than all eleven of Brazil's '58 team put together, who were some of the greatest artists in the history of soccer.

The stars of yesteryear were identified with a local club. Pelé was from Santos, Garrincha was from Botafogo, and Didi as well despite a fleeting experience overseas, and you could not imagine them without those colors or the yellow of the national team. That's the way it was in Brazil and everywhere else, thanks to loyalty to the uniform or clauses in the contracts of feudal servitude that until recently tied players for life. In France, for example, clubs had property rights over players until they were thirty-four years old; they could go free once they were all washed up. Demanding freedom, France's players joined the demonstrations of May 1968, when Paris barricades shook the world. They were led by Raymond Kopa.

The End of the Match

The ball turns, the world turns. People suspect the sun is a burning ball that works all day and spends the night bouncing around the heavens while the moon does its shift, though science is somewhat doubtful. There is absolutely no question, however, that the world turns around a spinning ball: the final of the '94 World Cup was watched by more than two billion people, the largest crowd ever of the many that have assembled in this planet's history. It is the passion most widely shared: many admirers of the ball play with her on fields and pastures, and many more have box seats in front of the TV and bite their nails as twenty-two men in shorts chase a ball and kick her to prove their love.

At the end of the '94 Cup every child born in Brazil was named Romário, and the turf of the stadium in Los Angeles was sold off like pizza, at twenty dollars a slice. A bit of insanity worthy of a better cause? A primitive and vulgar business? A bag of tricks manipulated by the owners? I'm one of those who believe that soccer might be all that, but it is also much more: a feast for the eyes that watch it and a joy for the body that plays it. A reporter once asked German theologian Dorothee Sölle, "How would you explain happiness to a child?"

"I wouldn't explain it," she answered. "I'd toss him a ball and let him play."

Professional soccer does everything to castrate that energy of happiness, but it survives in spite of all the spites. And maybe that's why soccer never stops being astonishing. As my friend Ángel Ruocco says, that's the best thing about it—its stubborn capacity for surprise. The more the technocrats program it down to the smallest detail, the more the powerful manipulate it, soccer continues to be the art of the unforeseeable. When you least expect it, the impossible occurs, the dwarf teaches the giant a lesson, and a runty, bowlegged black man makes an athlete sculpted in Greece look ridiculous.

An astonishing void: official history ignores soccer. Contemporary history texts fail to mention it, even in passing, in countries where soccer has been and continues to be a primordial symbol of collective identity. I play therefore I am: a style of play is a way of being that reveals the unique profile of each community and affirms its right to be different. Tell me how you play and I'll tell you who you are. For many years soccer has been played in different styles, unique expressions of the personality of each people, and the preservation of that diversity seems to me more

244 ⚽ ⚽ ⚽ ⚽ ⚽ ⚽ ⚽ ⚽ ⚽ ⚽ ⚽ ⚽ ⚽ ⚽

necessary today than ever before. These are days of obligatory uniformity, in soccer and everything else. Never has the world been so unequal in the opportunities it offers and so equalizing in the habits it imposes. In this end-of-century world, whoever does not die of hunger dies of boredom.

For years I have felt challenged by the memory and reality of soccer, and I have tried to write something worthy of this great pagan mass able to speak such different languages and unleash such universal passion. By writing, I was going to do with my hands what I never could accomplish with my feet: irredeemable klutz, disgrace of the playing fields, I had no choice but to ask of words what the ball I so desired denied me.

From that challenge, and from that need for expiation, this book was born. Homage to soccer, celebration of its lights, denunciation of its shadows. I don't know if it has turned out the way soccer would have liked, but I know it grew within me and has reached the final page, and now that it is born it is yours. And I feel that irreparable melancholy we all feel after making love and at the end of the match.

In Montevideo, in the summer of 1995

Extra Time

The 1998 World Cup

I ndia and Pakistan were fulfilling the dream of having their own bombs, waltzing into the great powers' exclusive nuclear club through the front door. Asian stock markets were lying prostrate, as was the long dictatorship of Suharto in Indonesia, emptied of power even while his pockets remained heavy with the $16 billion that power had placed there.

The world was losing Frank Sinatra, "The Voice." Eleven European countries were agreeing to launch a single currency, the euro. Well-informed sources in Miami were announcing the imminent fall of Fidel Castro, it was only a matter of hours.

João Havelange was abdicating the throne and installing in his place the dauphin Joseph Blatter, senior courtier in the kingdom of world soccer. General Videla, Argentina's former dictator who twenty years earlier had inaugurated the World Cup alongside Havelange, was marching off to jail, while in France a new championship got under way.

Despite serious complications caused by a strike at Air France, thirty-two teams arrived at elegant Saint Denis stadium to take part in the final World Cup of the century: fifteen from Europe, eight from the Americas, five from Africa, two from the Middle East, and two from Asia.

Cries of victory, murmurs of mourning: a month of combat in packed stadiums left France, the host, and Brazil, the favorite, waiting to cross swords in the final. Brazil lost 3–0. Suker from Croatia led the list of scorers with six, followed by Batistuta from Argentina and Vieri from Italy with five apiece.

According to a study reported in the London *Daily Telegraph*, during a soccer match fans secrete nearly as much testosterone as the players. Multinational companies also work up such a lather that you would think they were the ones on the field. Brazil did not become a five-time winner, but Adidas did. Beginning with the '54 Cup, which Adidas won with Germany, this was the fifth victory of the players representing the three bars. With France, Adidas raised the solid gold trophy once more. And with Zinedine Zidane, it took the prize for best player. Rival Nike, whose star, Ronaldo, was ill for the final, had to settle for second and fourth places, which it won with Brazil and the Netherlands. A junior company, Lotto, scored a coup with Croatia, which had never been to a World Cup and against all odds came in third.

Afterward, the grass at Saint Denis was sold off in slices, just as at the previous Cup in Los Angeles. The author of this book has no loaves of lawn to sell, but he would like to offer, free of charge, a few morsels of soccer that also had something to do with this championship.

Stars

The most famous soccer players are products who sell products. Back in Pelé's day, players played and that was all, or nearly all. By Maradona's time, television and advertising already held sway and things had changed. Maradona charged a high price and paid one as well. He charged for his legs, and paid with his soul.

At fourteen, Ronaldo was a poor mulatto from the slums of Rio de Janeiro, with rabbit teeth and the legs of a great striker, who couldn't play for Flamengo because he did not have the bus fare. At twenty-two he was making a thousand dollars an hour, even while he slept. Overwhelmed by his own popularity and the pressure of money, obliged to always shine and always win, Ronaldo suffered a nervous breakdown with violent convulsions hours before the '98 Cup was decided. They say Nike forced him to take the field in the final against France. He played but he didn't. And he could not demonstrate the virtues of Nike's new line of shoes, the R-9, being marketed on his feet.

Prices

At the end of the century, soccer reporters write less about players' abilities and more about the prices they command. Club presidents, businessmen, contractors, and related fishmongers crowd the soccer columns. Until a few years ago "pass" referred to the movement of the ball from one player to another. Now it alludes more to the movement of a player from one club to another, or one country to another. What's the return on investment in the stars? Soccer columnists bombard us with the vocabulary of the times: offer, buyout, option to buy, sale, foreclosure, appreciation, depreciation. During the 1998 World Cup, TV screens across the globe were invaded and overwhelmed by collective emotion, the most collective of emotions. But they were also turned into tradeshow displays. There were ups and downs in leg futures.

Hired Feet

Joseph Blatter, soccer's new monarch, gave an interview to the Brazilian magazine *Placar* at the end of 1995, while he was still Havelange's right-hand man. The journalist asked about the international players union being organized.

"FIFA doesn't deal with players," Blatter responded. "Players are employees of the clubs."

While Blatter the bureaucrat offered his disdain, there was good news for the athletes and for all of us who believe in human rights and freedom for labor. In a suit brought by Belgian soccer player Jean-Marc Bosman, Europe's highest judicial authority, the European Court of Justice, ruled that European players could become free agents at the end of their contracts.

Later on, Brazil's "Pelé Law" further weakened the chains of feudal servitude. But in many countries, players are still treated as fixed assets of the clubs, most of which are companies disguised as nonprofit organizations.

Just before the '98 Cup, one manager, Pacho Maturana, offered this opinion: "Nobody thinks about players' rights." That continues to be a truth as large as a house and as vast as the world, even though at long last players are winning the right to free agency. The higher a player goes in professional soccer, the greater are his obligations, always more numerous than his rights. He must live by the decisions of others, suffer military discipline, exhausting training, and incessant travel, and play day after day after day, always in top form, producing ever more.

When Winston Churchill reached the age of ninety, buoyant as ever, a journalist asked him the secret of his good health. "Sports," Churchill responded. "I never played them."

Advertisements

In today's world, everything that moves and everything that doesn't carries some sort of commercial message. Every soccer player is a billboard in movement, but FIFA expressly prohibits players from wearing messages of solidarity. Julio Grondona, the boss of Argentine soccer, reminded us all of this in 1997, when a few players tried to show their support for the demands of the country's teachers, who earn salaries of perpetual fasting. Not long before that, FIFA fined the English player Robbie Fowler for the crime of writing on his shirt a slogan in support of striking stevedores.

Roots

Many of soccer's greatest stars suffer discrimination because they are black or mulatto. On the field they find an alternative to the life of crime to which they had been condemned by statistical average, and thus they become symbols of collective hope.

A recent survey in Brazil showed that two out of three professional players never finished primary school. Many of these—half—have black or brown skin. Despite the invasion of the middle class evident lately on the field, Brazilian soccer today is not very different from the days of Pelé, who as a child used to steal peanuts in the train station.

Africans

Njanka, from Cameroon, took off from the back, left the entire population of Austria in the dust, and scored the prettiest goal of the '98 Cup. But Cameroon itself did not go far.

When Nigeria, with its joyous soccer, defeated the Spanish team, and Paraguay fought Spain to a tie, Spain's President José

María Aznar commented, "Even a Nigerian, even a Paraguayan could take your place." Then, when Nigeria was knocked out of the running, an Argentine commentator decreed, "They're all bricklayers, not one of them uses his head to think."

FIFA, which gives awards for fair play, did not play fair with Nigeria. Even though the team had just won the Olympics, they would not let it be seeded at the top of its group.

Black Africa's teams left the World Cup early, but Africa's children and grandchildren continued to shine on the teams of the Netherlands, France, Brazil, and others. Some commentators called them darkies. They never called the others whiteys.

Fervor

In April 1997 guerrillas occupying the Japanese embassy in the city of Lima were gunned down. When commandos burst in and carried out their spectacular lightning butchery, the guerrillas were playing soccer. Their leader, Néstor Cerpa Cartolini, died wearing the colors of Alianza, the club he loved.

Few things happen in Latin America that do not have some direct or indirect relation with soccer. Whether a shared celebration or a shipwreck that takes us all down, soccer counts in Latin America, sometimes more than anything else, even if the ideologues who love humanity but can't stand people don't realize it.

Latin Americans

Mexico played well in the '98 Cup. Paraguay and Chile were tough bones to chew. Colombia and Jamaica gave it their best. Brazil and Argentina gave it a lot less than their best, handcuffed by strategies that were rather stingy in joy and fantasy. On the Argentine squad all joy and fantasy fell to Ortega, master of gambols and arabesques but a crummy actor when it comes to rolling on the ground.

Dutch

Of the Latin American teams, to tell the truth, the one I liked best was the Netherlands. The orange offered a feast for the eyes, with good footwork and quick passes, luxuriating in the ball. Their style was due, in large part, to the contribution of players from South America, descendants of slaves born in Suriname.

There were no blacks among the ten thousand Dutch fans who traveled to France, but there certainly were on the field: Kluivert, Seedorf, Reiziger, Winter, Bogarde, Davids. The engine of the team, Davids plays and makes plays: he gets his goals and gets in trouble, because he will not accept that black players earn less than white ones.

French

Nearly all of the players wearing blue shirts and singing "La Marseillaise" before each match were immigrants or the children of immigrants. Thuram—elevated to the category of national hero for two magnificent goals—and Henry, Desailly, Vieira, and Karembeu were from Africa, the Caribbean, or New Caledonia. Most of the others came from Basque, Armenian, or Argentine families.

Zidane, the one most acclaimed, is the son of Algerians. "Zidane for President" wrote an anonymous hand on the Arc de Triomphe the day of the victory celebration. President? There are many Arabs and children of Arabs in France, but not a single one is a member of parliament, much less a minister.

A poll published during the World Cup found that four out of every ten people in France have racist views. Racism's doublespeak lets you cheer the heroes and curse the rest. France's victory was celebrated by a crowd comparable only to the one that overflowed the streets half a century ago, when the German occupation finally ended.

Fish

In 1997 an advertisement on Fox Sports exhorted viewers to watch soccer: "See the big fish gobble up the little ones." An invitation to boredom. Fortunately, on more than one occasion during the '98 Cup, the little fish ate the big ones, bones and all. That's the bright side we sometimes see in soccer, and in life.

The 2002 World Cup

Aseason of collapses. A terrorist attack had leveled the Twin Towers in New York. President Bush had rained missiles down upon Afghanistan and razed the dictatorship of the Taliban, which his father and Reagan had suckled. The war against terrorism was giving its blessing to military terror. Israeli tanks were demolishing Gaza and the West Bank, so that the Palestinians could continue paying for the Holocaust they did not commit.

Spider-Man was toppling box-office records. Well-informed sources in Miami were announcing the imminent fall of Fidel Castro, it was only a matter of hours. What did tumble was Argentina, the model nation, and down with it went its currency, government, and everything else. In Venezuela, a coup d'état overthrew President Chávez and, when a multitude reimposed the deposed leader, television, that champion of the free press, made like it had not heard.

Shattered by its own swindles, the corporate giant Enron, one of the more generous donors to the campaigns of Bush and most US senators, came crashing down. And like dominos, the stock of other sacred monsters went tumbling after: WorldCom, Xerox, Vivendi, Merck—all because of a few small billion-dollar accounting errors. FIFA's largest business partners, ISL and Kirch, were also going belly-up, but their outrageous bankruptcies failed to keep Joseph Blatter from being installed, by a landslide, on the throne of world soccer. If you want to look good, find someone worse: a master at cooking books and buying votes, Blatter the untouchable turned Havelange into a Sister of Charity.

Bertie Felstead was tumbling too, done in by death. Felstead, the oldest man in England, was the sole survivor of that extraordinary soccer match between British and German soldiers on Christmas Day 1915 in no-man's-land. Under the magical influence of a ball that appeared from who knows where, the battlefield became a playing field for a short while, until screaming officers managed to remind the soldiers that they were obliged to hate each other.

* * *

Thirty-two teams traveled to Japan and Korea to wage the seventeenth World Cup in the shiny new stadiums of twenty cities. The first World Cup of the new millennium was the first to be played in Asia. Pakistani children sewed the high-tech ball for Adidas that started rolling on opening night in the stadium at Seoul: a rubber chamber, surrounded by a cloth net covered with foam, all inside a skin of white polymer decorated with the symbol of fire. A ball built to lure fortunes from the grass.

* * *

There were two world soccer championships: one had athletes of flesh and blood; the other, held simultaneously, featured robots. The mechanical players, programmed by software engineers, waged RoboCup 2002 in the Japanese port of Fukuoka, across from the Korean coast. What do the businessmen, technocrats, bureaucrats, and ideologues of the soccer industry dream about? Theirs is a recurring dream, ever more like reality, in which players imitate robots.

Sad sign of the times: the twenty-first century sanctifies uniformity in the name of efficiency and sacrifices freedom on the altar of success. "You win not because you're good, rather you're good because you win," noted Cornelius Castoriadis some years ago. He wasn't referring to soccer, but he might as well have been. Wasting time is forbidden, so is losing. Reduced to a job, subjected to the laws of profitability, the game is no longer played. Like everything else, professional soccer seems to be run by the almighty, even if nonexistent, UEB (Union of the Enemies of Beauty).

Obedience, speed, strength, and none of those fancy turns: this is the mold into which globalization pours the game. Soccer gets mass-produced, and it comes out colder than a freezer and as merciless as a meat grinder: soccer for robots. Such boredom supposedly means progress, but historian Arnold Toynbee had already seen enough of that when he wrote, "Civilizations in decline are consistently characterized by a tendency towards standardization and uniformity."

* * *

Back to the flesh-and-blood Cup. In the opening match, more than one quarter of humanity witnessed the first surprise on television. France, winner of the previous championship, got beaten by Senegal, one of its former colonies and a first-time participant in the World Cup. Contrary to all predictions, France was sidelined in the first round without scoring a single goal. Argentina, the other great favorite, also fell in the first exchange. And then Italy and Spain were sent packing after suffering armed assaults at the hands of the referees. All these powerful teams were done in by twin brothers: the imperative of winning and the terror of losing. The greatest stars of world soccer came to the Cup overwhelmed by the weight of fame and responsibility, and exhausted from the ferocious pace demanded by the clubs for which they play.

With no World Cup history, no stars, no obligation to win or trepidation about losing, Senegal played in a state of grace and was the revelation of the championship. China, Ecuador, and Slovenia also faced a baptism by fire, but were sidelined in the first round. Senegal made it to the quarterfinals undefeated and no further, but their unending dance brought home a simple truth that tends to escape the scientists of the ball: soccer is a game, and those who really play it feel happy and make us happy too. The goal I liked best in the entire tournament was scored by Senegal: backheel by Thiaw, deft shot by Camara. Another Senegalese, Diouf, dribbled the ball an average of eight times per match, in a championship where that pleasure for the eyes seemed prohibited.

The other surprise was Turkey. Nobody could believe it. The country had been absent from the Cup for half a century. In its first match, against Brazil, the Turkish side was high-handedly cheated by the referee, but the team kept flying and ended up winning third place. Its fervor and quality play rendered the experts who had scorned it speechless.

Nearly all the rest was one long yawn. Fortunately, in its final matchups Brazil remembered that it was Brazil. The team finally let go and played like Brazilians, slipping out of the cage of efficient mediocrity in which the manager, Scolari, had locked them. Then their four R's, Rivaldo, Ronaldo, Ronaldinho, and Roberto Carlos, shone brilliantly, and Brazil at last turned into a fiesta.

* * *

And they were champions. Just before the final, 170 million Brazilians stuck pins in German sausages, and Germany succumbed 2–0. It was Brazil's seventh victory in seven matches. The two countries had each been finalists many times, but never before had they faced each other in the World Cup. Turkey took third place, South Korea fourth. Translated into market terms, Nike took first and fourth, while Adidas came in second and third.

The Brazilian Ronaldo, recovered after a long injury, led the list of scorers with eight, followed by his compatriot Rivaldo and Germany's Klose each with five, then the Dane Tomasson and the Italian Vieri with four goals apiece. Şükür of Turkey scored the fastest goal in World Cup history, eleven seconds after the match began.

For the very first time, a goalkeeper, the German Oliver Khan, was chosen as best player of the tournament. Such was the terror he inspired that his opponents thought he was a son of that other Khan, Genghis. But he wasn't.

The 2006 World Cup

As usual, CIA aircraft were flying in and out of Europe without permission or notice or so much as a hello–good-bye, ferrying prisoners to torture chambers around the world.

As usual, Israel was invading Gaza, and in order to rescue a soldier held hostage was holding Palestine's freedom hostage with guns blazing.

As usual, scientists were warning that the climate was coming unhinged and sooner rather than later the polar icecaps would melt and the oceans would swallow seaports and shorelines. But the ones poisoning the atmosphere and unhinging the climate continued, as usual, to turn a deaf ear.

As usual, the fix was in on the Mexican election, where the computer system for the official vote count was impeccably programmed by the brother-in-law of the candidate of the right.

As usual, well-informed sources in Miami were announcing the imminent fall of Fidel Castro, it was only a matter of hours.

As usual, human rights violations in Cuba were making head-lines. This time at the US military base in Guantánamo, where three of the hundreds of prisoners held without charge or trial were found hanged in their cells. The White House said the terrorists were just trying to attract attention.

As usual, a scandal was erupting after Evo Morales, the first in-digenous president of Bolivia, nationalized the country's oil and gas resources, thus committing the unpardonable crime of keeping his promises.

As usual, killings were continuing in Iraq, a country guilty of harboring oil, while Pandemic Studios of California was announc-ing a new video game in which the heroes invade Venezuela, also guilty of harboring oil.

And the United States was threatening to invade Iran, yet an-other country guilty of harboring oil. Iran was a menace because it wanted a nuclear bomb. Remind me, was it Iran that dropped the bomb on Hiroshima and Nagasaki?

Bruno, too, was a menace. Reared in captivity in Italy then re-leased, the bear was frolicking in the forests of Germany. Al-though he showed not the slightest interest in soccer, the agents of order were taking no chances. They shot Bruno to death in Bavaria just before the opening of the eighteenth World Cup.

* * *

Thirty-two countries from five continents played sixty-four matches in twelve attractive, well-designed, even majestic stadi-ums across a unified Germany: eleven in the West and just one in the East.

This World Cup had a theme: before each match the players unveiled a banner decrying the global plague of racism.

A hot topic: on the eve of the tournament, French political leader Jean-Marie Le Pen declared that the country could not see itself in its players, for nearly all were black, and he added that its captain Zinedine Zidane, more Algerian than French, refused to sing the national anthem. The vice president of the Italian senate, Roberto Calderoli, echoed the sentiment saying that the French

team consisted of blacks, Islamists, and Communists who preferred "l'Internationale" to "La Marseillaise" and Mecca to Bethle-
hem. Earlier, the coach of the Spanish team, Luis Aragonés, called
French player Thierry Henry a "black piece of shit," and the president in perpetuity of South American soccer, Nicolás Leoz,
opened his autobiography by saying he had been born "in a town
populated by thirty people and a hundred Indians."

At the end of the tournament, in practically the final moment
of the final match, a bull charged: Zidane, who was saying
farewell to soccer, head-butted a rival who had been needling him
with the sort of insult that lunatic fans like to shriek from the upper decks. The insulter got flattened and the insulted got a red
card from the referee and jeers from a crowd poised until then to
give him an ovation. And Zidane left the field for good.

Still, this was his World Cup. He was the best player of the
tournament, despite that final act of insanity or integrity, depending on how you look at it. Thanks to his beautiful moves, thanks
to his melancholy elegance, we could still believe that soccer was
not irredeemably condemned to mediocrity.

* * *

In that final match, shortly after Zidane was sent off, Italy
beat France on penalties and was crowned champion.

Until 1968 ties were decided by the toss of a coin, since then
by penalty shots: more or less another way of leaving it to chance.
France was better than Italy, but a few seconds obliterated more
than two hours of play. The same thing had happened in the
match that put Argentina, a better team than Germany, on the
plane home.

* * *

Eight players from the Italian club Juventus reached the final
in Berlin: five for Italy and three for France. Juventus was the club
most deeply implicated in the rackets uncovered on the eve of the
Cup. Italy's "Clean Hands" campaign became "Clean Feet":

judges found evidence of a vast array of deceptions, including paying off referees, buying journalists, falsifying contracts, cooking the books, raffling off positions, manipulating TV coverage . . . Also implicated was Milan, property of Silvio Berlusconi, the virtuoso who has so successfully avoided prosecution for his fraudulent practices in soccer, in business, and in government.

* * *

Italy won its fourth Cup and France came second, followed by Germany and Portugal. You might say Puma won out over Adidas and Nike.

Miroslav Klose of the German team was top scorer with five goals.

South America and Europe were tied: each continent had won the Cup nine times.

For the first time in history the same referee, Horacio Elizondo, blew the opening whistle in the inaugural match and the closing whistle in the final. He proved to be the right choice.

Other records were set, all of them Brazilian. Ronaldo, chubby but effective, became the highest scorer in World Cup history; Cafú became the player to win the most matches; and Brazil became the country with the most goals scored (an astounding 201) as well as the country with the most consecutive victories (an equally astounding eleven).

Nevertheless, in the 2006 World Cup Brazil was present but not visible. Superstar Ronaldinho provided neither goals nor glamour, and angry fans transformed a twenty-foot statue of him into a pile of ashes and twisted steel.

* * *

By the final stages, the tournament had become a Eurocup without a single Latin American, African, or any other non-European team.

Not much imagination was on display. Except for the Ecuadoran team, which played beautifully even if to little effect, this was a World Cup without surprises. As one spectator summed it up: "The players were on their best behavior. They didn't smoke, they didn't drink, they didn't play."

Artists made way for weight lifters and Olympic runners who every once in a while kicked a ball or an opponent.

The strategy now embraced as common sense paid off: nearly everyone back, practically no one forward; the Great Wall of China defending the goal and the Lone Ranger hoping for a breakaway. Only a few years ago teams played five men forward. Now there is but one, and at this rate we'll soon be down to none.

Argentina's cartooning zoologist, Roberto Fontanarrosa, drew the inevitable conclusion: strikers are like pandas, an endangered species.

The 2010 World Cup

Iran was fast becoming the gravest threat to humankind, thanks to an international campaign declaring it might have or maybe even does have nuclear weapons, *as if* it had been the Iranians who dropped the bomb on civilians in Hiroshima and Nagasaki.

Ships in international waters carrying food, medicine, and toys to Palestine were being machine-gunned in one of the habitual criminal acts by which Israel punishes the Palestinians, *as if* they, who are Semites, were to blame for anti-Semitism and its horrors.

The International Monetary Fund, the World Bank, and numerous governments were humiliating Greece, obliging the country to accept the unacceptable, *as if* the Greeks, and not the bankers of Wall Street, were responsible for the worst international crisis since 1929.

The Pentagon was proclaiming joyfully that in Afghanistan its experts had discovered a trillion dollars' worth, of gold, cobalt, copper, iron, and especially lithium, the coveted essential ingredient in cell phones and laptops, *as if* after nearly nine years of war and thousands of deaths the invading country had finally found what it was looking for in the country it had invaded.

In Colombia a common grave was revealing more than two thousand nameless bodies that the army had thrown there *as if* they were guerrillas slain in combat, although people living nearby knew they were union members, community activists, and peasants defending their lands.

One of the worst ecological catastrophes of all time was turning the Gulf of Mexico into an immense puddle of oil, and a month and a half after it began, the petro-volcano at the bottom of the sea was still in full eruption and the company responsible, British Petroleum, was still whistling and looking the other way, *as if* it had played no part in the disaster.

In several countries, a flood of accusations of sexual abuse and child rape was inundating the Catholic Church, and traumas hitherto repressed by fear were coming to light everywhere, while certain ecclesiastical sources were defending themselves by saying that such atrocities also occurred outside the Church, *as if* that could excuse it, and by claiming that in many cases the priests had been provoked, *as if* the victims were the guilty parties.

Well-informed sources in Miami were still denying that Fidel Castro was alive and kicking, *as if* he weren't giving them new cause for bitterness every day.

Two irreplaceable writers were taking their leave, José Saramago and Carlos Monsiváis, and we missed them *as if* we did not know they would keep returning from the dead just for the joy of tormenting the owners of the world.

And in the port of Hamburg, a multitude was celebrating the return to Germany's first division of the St. Pauli soccer club, which, impossible as it seems, has twenty million fans under the club motto: "Say No to Racism, No to Sexism, No to Homophobia, No to Nazism."

Meanwhile, far away from there, in South Africa, the nineteenth World Cup got under way, wrapped in one of those banners: "Say No to Racism."

* * *

For a month the world stopped spinning and many of its inhabitants stopped breathing.

Nothing out of the ordinary, since this occurs every four years, but what was extraordinary was that this was the first World Cup held on African soil.

Black Africa, scorned, condemned to silence and oblivion, could bask in the spotlight of world attention, at least for the short while the championship lasted.

Thirty-two countries did battle in ten stadiums that cost a fortune. Nobody knows how South Africa will manage to keep those concrete behemoths running, a multi-million-dollar extravagance easy to explain but hard to justify in one of the most unjust countries in the world.

* * *

The most beautiful of the stadiums, in the shape of a flower, opened its immense petals above a bay named for Nelson Mandela.

This World Cup was a well-deserved homage to the founder of South Africa's democracy. The fruits of Mandela's labors can be seen in one way or another all over the globe. Nevertheless, in his country blacks are still the poorest and the most punished by police and plagues, and black were the beggars, prostitutes, and street kids who on the eve of the Cup were hidden from view to ensure that visitors did not get a bad impression.

* * *

Throughout the tournament, one could see that African soccer had conserved its agility but lost its inventiveness and daring, lots of running but little dancing. There are those who believe the managers, nearly all of them from Europe, cast a chilling effect. If true, they did scant favor for a soccer that promised so much exuberance.

Africa sacrificed its flair in the name of efficacy, and efficacy shone by its absence. Only one African country, Ghana, came to be among the eight best; and soon Ghana too was sent home. Not a single African team survived, not even the hosts.

Many African players worthy of their heritage of good soccer live and play on the continent that enslaved their ancestors.

In one of the World Cup matches, the Boateng brothers, sons of a Ghanaian father, played against each other: one in a Ghanaian shirt, the other in a German one.

Of the players on the Ghanaian side, not a one played in Ghana's national championship.

Of the players on the German side, every single one played in Germany's national championship.

Like Latin America, Africa exports working hands and working feet.

* * *

"Jabulani" was the name of the soapy, half-crazed tournament ball that eluded hands and flouted feet. The World Cup was obliged to embrace this novelty from Adidas, even though the players did not like it one bit. From their castle in Zurich, the owners of soccer do not propose, they impose. That's their way.

* * *

The errors and horrors committed by certain officials made obvious what common sense has for many years demanded.

Common sense cries out, always in vain, to allow the referee to check the video replay on decisive but questionable plays. Technology now permits a consultation that is as quick and easy as a glance at that other technological instrument the referee uses to measure the length of the match. It's called a clock.

Every other sport—basketball, tennis, baseball, swimming, even fencing and car racing—makes regular use of electronic assistance. Not soccer. And the explanation of its owners would be comical if it were not suspiciously convenient: "Mistakes are part of the game," they say, and we are left slack-jawed at the revelation that *errare humanum est.*

* * *

The best save of the tournament was the work of a goal scorer, not a goalkeeper: Uruguayan striker Luis Suárez, standing on the goal line in the final minute of a decisive match, blocked the slippery ball with both hands. A goal would have taken his country out of the Cup; thanks to his act of patriotic lunacy, Suárez was sent packing but Uruguay was not.

* * *

Uruguay, which entered the World Cup behind everyone else after a painful qualifying round, played the entire championship without ever giving an inch and was the only Latin American country to reach the semifinals. In the Uruguayan press, several cardiologists warned that "excessive joy can damage the heart." Many of us Uruguayans embraced the chance to die of something other than boredom, and the country's streets became a fiesta. After all, the right to celebrate one's own merits is always preferable to the pleasure some derive from the misfortune of others.

Uruguay ended up in fourth place, not bad for the only country that kept this World Cup from becoming a European championship.

Diego Forlán, our striker, was chosen as best player of the tournament.

* * *

Spain won. A country that had never held the trophy won it cleanly thanks to the marvels of its soccer of solidarity, all for one and one for all, and to the astonishing abilities of a tiny magician named Andrés Iniesta.

The Netherlands came in second, after a final match that gave its finest traditions a swift kick in the pants.

* * *

The first- and second-place finishers of the previous World Cup returned home without even opening their suitcases. In 2006 Italy and France met in the final match. This time they met in the airport departure lounge. In Italy, more and more voices clamored against a soccer played to keep the other side from playing. In France, the disaster provoked a political crisis and set off racist outrage, since nearly all the players who sang "La Marseillaise" in South Africa's stadiums were black.

Other favorites, like England, did not last long either.

Brazil and Argentina suffered cruel humiliations. Brazil was unrecognizable, except for the few moments when the team slipped free of the cage of its own defensive plan. What was the illness that required such a dubious remedy?

Germany rained goals on Argentina in their final match. Half a century before, other Argentine players were pummeled by coins when they returned from a disastrous performance, but this time they were welcomed by an adoring crowd. There are still people who believe in things more important than winning or losing.

* * *

This World Cup confirmed the remarkable frequency with which players get injured, crushed by the exhausting pace professional soccer imposes with impunity. One could say some stars have grown rich, even fantastically rich, but that is only true for a select few who, besides playing two or more matches a week and besides training night and day, must sacrifice their scant free time to the demands of consumer society, selling underwear, cars, perfume, and shavers, or posing for the covers of glossy magazines. In the end, it only proves this world is so absurd we even have slaves who are millionaires.

* * *

The two most highly publicized and anticipated superstars missed their appointments. Lionel Messi wanted to be there, did what he could, and something shone through. They say Cristiano Ronaldo was there, but no one saw him; perhaps he was too busy looking at himself.

But a new star emerged from the depths of the sea and rose unexpectedly to the topmost heights of the soccer firmament. He's an octopus and he lives in an aquarium in Germany. His name is Paul, though he deserves to be called Octodamus.

Before each match, he made his prophecies. They gave him a choice of two mussels bearing the flags of the two opponents. He ate the mussels of the winners and was never wrong.

The octo-oracle, who had a decisive influence on the betting, was listened to with religious reverence in the soccer world, and was loved and hated and even slandered by certain resentful souls like me. When he announced that Uruguay would lose to Germany, I accused: "This octopus has been bought off."

* * *

On the first day of the World Cup, I hung a sign on the door of my house that said: "Closed for soccer."

When I took it down a month later, I had played sixty-four matches, beer in hand, without budging from my favorite chair.

The exploit left me drained, muscles stiff, throat raw, but already I feel nostalgic. I miss the insufferable litany of the vuvuzelas, the emotion of those goals injurious to bad hearts, the beauty of the best plays repeated in slow motion. I miss the celebration and the mourning too, because sometimes soccer is a pleasure that hurts, and the music of a victory that sets the dead to dancing sounds a lot like the clamorous silence of an empty stadium, where one of the defeated, unable to move, still sits in the middle of the immense stands, alone.

Sources

Aguirre, José Fernando, *Ricardo Zamora* (Barcelona: Clíper, 1958).

Alcântara, Eurípides, "Aeficiencia da retranca," and other articles by Marcos Sá Corrêa, Maurício Cardoso and Roberto Pompeu de Toledo, special edition of *Veja* (São Paulo), July 18, 1994.

Altafini, José, *I magnifici 50 del calcio mondiale* (Milan: Sterling & Kupfer, 1985).

Anuario mundial de football professional (Buenos Aires), vol. 1, no. 1, June 1934.

Arias, Eduardo et al., *Colombia gol: De Pedernera a Maturana: Grandes momentos del fútbol* (Bogotá: Cerec, 1991).

Archetti, Eduardo P., "Estilo y virtudes masculinas en *El Gráfico: la creación del imaginario del fútbol argentino*," *Desarrollo Económico* 35, no. 139 (Oct.–Dec. 1995): 419–442.

Arucci, Daniel, "Mágicos templos del fútbol," *El Gráfico* (Buenos Aires), March 20, 1991.

Asociación del Fútbol Argentino, *Cien años con el fútbol* (Buenos Aires: Zago, 1993).

Associazione Italiana Arbitri, *75 anni di storia* (Milan: Vallardi, 1987).

Barba, Alejandro, *Foot Ball, Base Ball y Lawn Tennis* (Barcelona: Soler, n.d.).

Bartissol, Charles and Christophe, *Les racines du foot-ball français* (Paris: Pac, 1983).

Bayer, Osvaldo, *Fútbol argentino* (Buenos Aires: Sudamericana, 1990).

Benedetti, Mario, "Puntero izquierdo," in the anthology *Hinchas y goles: El fútbol como personaje* (Buenos Aires: Desde la Gente, 1994).

Blanco, Eduardo, "El negocio del fútbol," *La Maga* (Buenos Aires), December 7, 1994.

Boix, Jaume and Arcadio Espada, *El deporte del poder* (Madrid: Temas de Hoy, 1991).

Boli, Basile, *Black Boli* (Paris: Grasset, 1994).

Brie, Christian de, "Il calcio francese sotto i piedi dei mercanti," in *Le Monde Diplomatique* (Italian edition), June 1994, published by *Il Manifesto* (Rome).

Buford, Bill, *Among the Thugs: The Experience and the Seduction of Crowd Violence* (New York: Norton, 1992).

Camus, Albert, testimony published in Eduardo Galeano's anthology *Su majestad el fútbol* (Montevideo: Arca, 1994).

———, *Le premier homme* (Paris: Gallimard, 1994).

Cappa, Ángel, "Fútbol, un animal de dos patas," *Disenso* (Las Palmas, Canary Islands), no. 7.

Carías, Marco Virgilio with Daniel Slutzky, *La guerra inútil: Análisis socioeconómico del conflicto entre Honduras y El Salvador* (San José, Costa Rica: EDUCA, 1971).

Cepeda Samudio, Alvaro, "Garrincha," in *Alrededor del fútbol* (Medellín: University of Antioquia, 1994).

Cerretti, Franco, *Storia illustrata dei Mondiali di Calcio* (Rome: Anthropos, 1986).

Comisión de Asuntos Históricos, *La historia de Vélez Sarsfield (1910/1980)* (Buenos Aires, 1980).

Coutinho, Edilberto, *Maracanã, adeus* (Havana: Casa de las Américas, 1980).

Decaux, Sergio, *Peñarol campeón del mundo* (Montevideo: Colección "100 Años de Fútbol," no. 21, 1970).

Délano, Poli, ed., *Hinchas y goles: El fútbol como personaje* (Buenos Aires: Desde la Gente, 1994).

"Discurso de João Havelange ante la cámara de Comercio Brasil-USA en Nueva York, el 27 de octubre de 1994," *El Gráfico* (Buenos Aires), November 8, 1994.

Duarte, Orlando, *Todas las Copas del Mundo* (Madrid: McGraw-Hill, 1993).

Dujovne Ortiz, Alicia, *Maradona sono io:. Un viaggio alla scoperta di un aidentitá* (Naples: Edizioni Scientifiche Italiane, 1992).

Dunning, Eric, et al., *The Roots of Football Hooliganism* (London: Routledge & Kegan Paul, 1988).

"Entrevista con cuatro integrantes de la 'barrabrava' del club Nacional," *La República* (Montevideo), December 1, 1993.

Escande, Enrique, *Nolo: El fútbol de la cabeza a los pies* (Buenos Aires: Ukamar, 1992).

Faria, Octavio de, et al., *O ôlho na bola* (Rio de Janeiro: Gol, 1968).

Felice, Gianni de, "Il giallo della Fifa," *Guerin sportivo* (Turin), January 25, 1995.

Fernández, José Ramón, *El fútbol mexicano: ¿Un juego sucio?* (Mexico: Grijalbo, 1994).

Fernández Seguí, J.A., *La preparación física del futbolista europeo* (Madrid: Sanz Martínez, 1977).

Ferreira, Carlos, *A mi juego . . .* (Buenos Aires: La Campana, 1983).

Galiacho, Juan Luis, *Jesús Gil y Gil, el gran comediante* (Madrid: Temas de Hoy, 1993).

Gallado, César L., et al., *Los maestros* (Montevideo: Colección "100 Años de Fútbol," no. 12, 1970).

García Candau, Julián, *El fútbol sin ley* (Madrid: Penthalon, 1981).

——, *Épica y lírica del fútbol* (Madrid: Alianza, 1995).

Geronazzo, Argentino, *Técnica y táctica del fútbol* (Buenos Aires: Lidiun, 1980).

Gispert, Carlos, et al., *Enciclopedia mundial del fútbol*, 6 vols. (Barcelona: Océano, 1982).

Goethals, Raymond, *Le douzième homme* (Paris: Laffont, 1994).

Guevara, Ernesto, *Mi primer gran viaje* (Buenos Aires: Seix Barral, 1994).

Gutiérrez Cortinas, Eduardo, *Los negros en el fútbol uruguayo* (Montevideo: Colección "100 Años de Fútbol," no. 10, 1970).

Hernández Coronado, Pablo, *Las cosas del fútbol* (Madrid: Plenitud, 1955).

Herrera, Helenio, *Yo* (Barcelona: Planeta, 1962).

Herschmann, Micael, and Kátia Lerner, *Lance de sorte: O futebol e o jogo do bicho na Belle Epoque carioca* (Rio de Janeiro: Diadorim, 1993).

"Historia de la Copa del Mundo," documentary video and special series (Buenos Aires: El Gráfico, 1994).

"Historia del fútbol," three documentary videos (Madrid: Transworld International Metrovideo, 1991).

Howe, Don, and Brian Scovell, *Manual de fútbol* (Barcelona: Martínez Roca, 1991).

Hübener, Karl Ludolf, et al., *¿Nunca más campeón mundial? Seminario sobre fútbol, deportes y política en el Uruguay* (Montevideo: Fesur, 1990).

Huerta, Héctor, *Héroes de consumo popular* (Guadalajara: Agata, 1992).

274

Ichah, Robert, *Platini* (Paris: Inéditions, 1994).

"Interview with João Havelange," *The Times* (London), February 15, 1991.

Lago, Alessandro dal, *Descrizione di una battaglia: I rituali del calcio* (Bologna: Il Mulino, 1990).

——, with Roberto Moscati, *Regalateci un sogno: Miti e realtà del tifo calcistico in Italia* (Milan: Bompiani, 1992).

——, with Pier Aldo Rovatti, *Per gioco: Píccolo manuale dell/esperienza ludica* (Milan: Cortina, 1993).

La Maga (Buenos Aires), "Homenaje al fútbol argentino," special edition, Jan/Feb 1994.

Lazzarini, Marta, and Patricia Luppi, "Reportaje a Roberto Perfumo," in *Boletín de temas de psicología social* (Buenos Aires), vol. 2, no. 5, September 1991.

Lever, Janet, *La locurapor el fútbol* (Mexico: FCE, 1985).

"Lezioni di Storia," series of four supplements in *Il Manifesto* (Rome), June/July 1994.

Loedel, Carlos, *Hechos y actores del profesionalismo* (Montevideo: Colección "100 Años de Fútbol," no. 14, 1970).

Lombardo, Ricardo, *Donde se cuentan proezas: Fútbol uruguayo (1920/1930)* (Montevideo: Banda Oriental, 1993).

Lorente, Rafael, *Di Stéfano cuenta su vida* (Madrid: n.p., 1954).

Lorenzo, Juan Carlos, and Jorge Castelli, *El fútbol en un mundo de cambios* (Buenos Aires: Freeland, 1977).

Lucero, Diego, *La boina fantasma* (Montevideo: Colección "100 Años de Fútbol," no. 20, 1970).

Marelli, Roberto, *Estudiante de La Plata, campeón intercontinental* (Buenos Aires: Norte, 1978).

Mário Filho, *O romance do foot-ball* (Rio de Janeiro: Pongetti, 1949).

——, *O negro no futebol brasileiro* (Rio de Janeiro: Civilização Brasileira, 1964).

——, *Histórias do Flamengo* (Rio de Janeiro: Record, 1966).

——, *O sapo de Arubinha* (São Paulo: Companhia das Letras, 1994).

Martín, Carmelo, *Valdano: Sueños de fútbol* (Madrid: El País/Aguilar, 1994).

Maturana, Francisco, with José Clopatofsky, *Talla mundial* (Bogotá: Intermedio, 1994).

Mercier, Joseph, *Le football* (Paris: Presses Universitaires, 1979).

Meynaud, Jean, *Sport et politique* (Paris: Payot, 1966).

Milá, Mercedes, "La violencia en el fútbol," segment of television program *Queremos saber*, Antena 3 (Madrid), January 1993.

Miná, Gianni, "Le vie del calcio targate Berlusconi," *La Repubblica* (Rome), May 6, 1988.

——, "I padroni del calcio. La Federazione s' é fatta holding," *La Repubblica* (Rome), July 19, 1990.

——, with other members of "La classe non è acqua" committee, *Te Diegum* (Milan: Leonardo, 1991).

Morales, Franklin, "Historia de Nacional" and "Historia de Peñarol," supplements to *La Mañana* (Montevideo), 1989.

——, *Fútbol, mito y realidad* (Montevideo: Colección "Nuestra Tierra," no. 22, 1969).

——, *Los albores del fútbol uruguayo* (Montevideo: Colección "100 Años de Fútbol," no. 2, 1969).

——, *La gloria tan temida* (Montevideo: Colección "100 Años de Fútbol," no. 1, 1969).

——, *Enviado especial (1)* (Montevideo: Banco de Boston, 1994).

Morris, Desmond, *The Soccer Tribe* (London: Jonathan Cape, 1981).

Moura, Roberto, "Testimonios de Domingos da Guia y Didi," *Pesquisa de campo* (Universidad del Estado de Rio de Janeiro), June 1994.

Mura, Gianni, "Il calcio dei boia," *La Repubblica* (Rome), November 29, 1994.

Nogueira, Armando, et al., *A Copa que ninguém viu e a que não queremos lembrar* (São Paulo: Companhia das Letras, 1994).

Orwell, George, et al., *El fútbol* (Buenos Aires: Jorge Alvarez, 1967).

Ossa, Carlos, *La historia de Colo-Colo* (Santiago de Chile: Plan, 1971).

Panzeri, Dante, *Fútbol, dinámica de lo impensado* (Buenos Aires: Paidós, 1967).

Papa, Antonio, and Guido Panico, *Storia sociale del calcio in Italia* (Bologna: Il Mulino, 1993).

Pawson, Tony, *The Goalscorers: From Bloomer to Keegan* (London: Cassell, 1978).

Pedrosa, Milton (ed.), *Gol de letra* (Rio de Janeiro: Gol, n.d).

Pepe, Osvaldo, et al., *El libro de los Mundiales* (Buenos Aires: Crea, 1978).

Perdigão, Paulo, *Anatomía de uma derrota* (Porto Alegre: L&PM, 1986).

Peucelle, Carlos, *Fútbol todotiempo e historia de "La Máquina"* (Buenos Aires: Axioma, 1975).

Pippo, Antonio, *Obdulio desde el alma* (Montevideo: Fin de Siglo, 1993).

Platini, Michel, with Patrick Mahé, *Ma vie comme un match* (Paris: Laffont, 1987).

Ponte Preta, Stanislaw, *Bola na rede: A batalha do bi* (Rio de Janeiro: Civilização Brasileira, 1993).

Poveda Márquez, Fabio, *El Pibe: De pescaíto a la gloria* (Bogotá: Intermedio, 1994).

Puppo, Julio César, "El Hachero," *Nueve contra once* (Montevideo: Arca, 1976).

——, *Crónicas de fútbol* (Montevideo: Enciclopedia Uruguaya, 1969).

Rafael, Eduardo, "Memoria: José Manuel Moreno," *El Toque* (Buenos Aires), March 17, 1994.

Ramírez, Miguel Ángel, "Los cachirules: la historia detrás de la nota," *Revista mexicana de comunicación*, no. 1, Sept./Oct. 1988.

——, "Emilio Maurer contra Televisa, una batalla épica en el fútbol local," *La Jornada* (Mexico), December 7–12, 1993.

Reid, Alastair, *Ariel y Calibán* (Bogotá: Tercer Mundo, 1994).

Ribeiro, Péris, *Didi, o gênio da folha seca* (Rio de Janeiro: Imago, 1993).

Rocca, Pablo, *Literatura y fútbol en el Uruguay (1899/1990)* (Montevideo: Arca, 1991).

Rodrigues, Nelson, *A sombra das chuteiras imortais* (São Paulo: Companhia das Letras, 1993).

——, *A patria em chuteiras* (São Paulo: Companhia das Letras, 1994).

——, with Mário Filho, *Fla-Flu* (Rio de Janeiro: Europa, 1987).

Rodríguez, Nelson, *El fútbol como apostolado* (Montevideo: Juventus/Colegio de Escribanos, 1995).

Rodríguez Arias, Miguel, "Diego" (video) (Buenos Aires: Las Patas de la Mentira, 1994).

Rowles, James, *El conflicto Honduras–El Salvador (1969)* (San José, Costa Rica: EDUCA, 1980).

Ruocco, Ángel, "Grandes equipos italianos en zozobra" (ANSA) *El País* (Montevideo), January 16, 1994.

Ryswick, Jacques de, *100,000 heures de football* (Paris: La Table Ronde, 1962).

Saldanha, João, *Meus amigos* (Rio de Janeiro: Nova Mitavaí, 1987).

——, *Futebol e outras histórias* (Rio de Janeiro: Record, 1988).

Salvo, Alfredo di, *Amadeo Carrizo* (Buenos Aires: n.p. 1992).

Sanz, Tomás, and Roberto Fontanarrosa, *Pequeño diccionario ilustrado del fútbol argentino* (Buenos Aires: Clarín/Aguilar, 1994).

Sasía, José, *Orsai en el paraíso* (Montevideo: La Pluma, 1992).

Scher, Ariel, and Héctor Palomino, *Fútbol: Pasión de multitudes y de elites* (Buenos Aires: Cisea, 1988).

Schumacher, Harald, *Der Anpfiff: Enthüllungen über den deutschen Fußball* (Munich: Knaur, 1987).

Scliar, Salomão (ed.), et al., *A história ilustrada do futebol brasileiro*, 4 vols. (São Paulo: Edobras, n.d).

Scopelli, Alejandro, *¡Hola, mister! El fútbol por dentro* (Barcelona: Juventud, 1957).

Seiferheld, Alfredo, and Pedro Servín Fabio, *Álbum fotográfico del fútbol paraguayo* (Asunción: Editorial Histórica, 1986).

Shakespeare, William, *The Comedy of Errors* (London: Methuen, 1907).

——, *King Lear* (London: Samuel French, 1967).

Shaw, Duncan, *Fútbol y franquismo* (Madrid: Alianza, 1987).

Silva, Thomaz Soares da, *Zizinho: O Mestre Ziza* (Rio de Janeiro: Maracaná, 1985).

Simson, Vyv, and Andrew Jennings, *Dishonored Games: Corruption, Money, and Greed at the Olympics* (New York: Shapolsky, 1992).

Smorto, Giuseppe, "Nazione corrotto, calcio infetto," *La Repubblica* (Rome), March 26, 1993.

Sobrequés, Jaume, *Historia del Fútbol Club Barcelona* (Barcelona: Labor, 1994).

Soriano, Osvaldo, *Cuentos de los años felices* (Buenos Aires: Sudamericana, 1994).

Souza, Roberto Pereira de, "O poderoso chefão," *Playboy* (Brazilian edition), May 1994.

Starosin, Andrei, *Por esas canchas de fútbol* (Moscow: Lenguas Extranjeras, 1959).

Suburú, Nilo J., *Al fútbol se juega así: Catorce verdades universales* (Montevideo: Tauro, 1968).

——, *Primer diccionario del fútbol* (Montevideo: Tauro, 1968).

Teissie, Justin, *Le football* (Paris: Vigot, 1969).

Termes, Josep, et al., *Onze del barça* (Barcelona: Columna, 1994).

Thibert, Jacques, *La fabuleuse histoire du football* (Paris: Odil, 1974).

Traverso, Jorge, *Primera línea* (Montevideo: Banco de Boston, 1992).

Uriarte, María Teresa, et al., *El juego de pelota en Mesoamérica: Raíces y supervivencia* (Mexico: Siglo XXI, 1992).

Valdano, Jorge, "Las ocurrencias de Havelange," *El País* (Madrid) May 28, 1990.

Verdú, Vicente, *El fútbol. Mitos, ritos y símbolos* (Madrid: Alianza, 1980).

Vinnai, Gerhard, *El fútbol como ideología* (Mexico: Siglo XXI, 1974).

Volpicelli, Luigi, *Industrialismo y deporte* (Buenos Aires: Paidós, 1967).

Wolstenholme, Kenneth, *Profesionales del fútbol* (Barcelona: Molino, 1969).

Zito Lema, Vicente, *Conversaciones con Enrique Pichon-Rivière* (Buenos Aires: Cinco, 1991).

Index

Iran, 174, 175, 259, 263Irangate,
193
Iraq, 194, 259
ISL Marketing, 168, 172, 254
Israel, 130, 154, 253, 258, 263
Italian Magicians Association,
73
Italy, 38, 62, 68, 69, 70, 73, 77,
78, 79, 80, 110, 113, 132,
139, 154, 157, 162, 175,
176, 180, 183, 184, 187,
188, 197, 201, 204, 208,
209, 215, 219, 223, 224,
227, 228, 234, 255, 259,
260, 261, 268
Ivanov, Valentin, 132
Ivory Coast, 214

Jabulani, 266
Jairzinho, 154, 155, 157
Jamaica, 250
Japan, 25, 170, 192, 254
Japan Airlines, 171
Jaramillo, Bernardo, 208
Jef United Ichihara, 170
Jennings, Andrew, 110
Jerkovic, Dražan, 132
John, Elton, 172
John XXIII, Pope, 114, 130
Jongbloed, Jan, 179
Joplin, Janis, 153
Joya, Juan, 146
Juventus, 170, 260

Karambeu, Christian, 251
Kashima, 171, 217
Keegan, Kevin, 186
Kempes, Mario, 158, 176
Khan, Oliver, 257
King Fahd Stadium, 20
Kipling, Rudyard, 36
Kirch, 254
Kissinger, Henry, 175
Kléber, 110
Klinsmann, Jurgen, 213, 224
Klose, Miroslav, 257, 261
Kluivert, Patrick, 251
Kocsis, Sandor, 40–1, 106
Kodak, 169
Koeman, Ronald, 204
Kopa, Raymond, 40, 115, 122,
187, 241
Krol, Ruud, 163, 179
Kubala, Ladislao, 40–1
Kuwait, 183, 184
La Paz, 229
La Plata, 147, 159
Labruna, Ángel, 86
Lacoste, Carlos Alberto, 178
Lagerkvist, Pär, 161
Lago, Pedro, 85
Lángara, Isidro, 40, 70
Langenus, John, 63
Lantos, Mihály, 107
Larylin, 109
Latin America, 39, 51, 63, 70, 89,
114, 182, 231, 250, 251

The Nation Institute

Nation.

Founded in 2000, **Nation Books** has become a leading voice in American independent publishing. The inspiration for the imprint came from the *Nation* magazine, the oldest independent and continuously published weekly magazine of politics and culture in the United States.

The imprint's mission is to produce authoritative books that break new ground and shed light on current social and political issues. We publish established authors who are leaders in their area of expertise, and endeavor to cultivate a new generation of emerging and talented writers. With each of our books we aim to positively affect cultural and political discourse.

Nation Books is a project of The Nation Institute, a nonprofit media center established to extend the reach of democratic ideals and strengthen the independent press. The Nation Institute is home to a dynamic range of programs: our award-winning Investigative Fund, which supports groundbreaking investigative journalism; the widely read and syndicated website TomDispatch; our internship program in conjunction with the *Nation* magazine; and Journalism Fellowships that fund up to 20 high-profile reporters every year.

For more information on Nation Books, the *Nation* magazine, and The Nation Institute, please visit:

www.nationbooks.org
www.nationinstitute.org
www.thenation.com
www.facebook.com/nationbooks.ny
Twitter: @nationbooks